Approaches to Adult ESL
Literacy Instruction

Marzoveinte?

Approaches to Adult ESL Literacy Instruction

JoAnn Crandall & Joy Kreeft Peyton, Editors

A co-publication of
the Center for Applied Linguistics and Delta Systems Co., Inc.
prepared by the National Clearinghouse for ESL Literacy Education,
an adjunct ERIC Clearinghouse

Language in Education

Theory & Practice

ERIC

CAL

CAL ©1993 by the Center for Applied Linguistics
and by Delta Systems Co., Inc.

Printed in the United States of America

10 9 8 7 6 5 4 3 2 1

Language in Education: Theory and Practice 82
Editorial/production supervision: Joy Peyton and Fran Keenan
Editorial assistance: Amy Fitch
Copyediting: Elizabeth Rangel
Interior design and production: Julie Booth and Sonia Kundert
Cover design and production: Vincent Sagart

ISBN   0-937354-82-1

This publication was prepared with funding from the Office of Educational Research and Improvement, U.S. Department of Education, under contract No. RI 89166001. The opinions expressed in this report do not necessarily reflect the positions or policies of OERI or ED.

Library of Congress Cataloging-in-Publication Data

Approaches to adult ESL literacy instruction / JoAnn Crandall & Joy
    Kreeft Peyton, editors.
        p.   cm. — (Language in education ; 82)
    "Prepared by the National Clearinghouse on Literacy Education, an
adjunct ERIC Clearinghouse."
    Includes bibliographical references.
    ISBN 0-937354-82-1
    1. English language—Study and teaching—Foreign speakers.
2. English language—Study and teaching—United States. 3. Adult
education—United States. I. Crandall, JoAnn. II. Peyton, Joy
Kreeft. III. National Clearinghouse on Literacy Education.
IV. Series.
PE1128.A2A58   1993
428' . 007—dc20   93-30665

Contents

Introduction

JoAnn Crandall

University of Maryland

Baltimore County

During the past decade, the subject of adult literacy has received increased attention around the world, culminating in the designation of 1990 as International Literacy Year and the convening of the World Conference on Education for All that same year in Thailand. In the United States, Canada, and many other countries, 1990 was also the occasion for a variety of educational commissions or task forces to plan for the year 2000. A major goal of all these endeavors was universal adult literacy.

Demographic, Economic, and Social Influences

Demographic, economic, and social factors all contribute to the urgency for enhanced adult literacy education in the United States. (See Chisman & Associates, 1990, for further discussion.) If we are to achieve the goal of universal adult literacy, a great deal more will need to be done, especially to meet the needs of the growing numbers of individuals who speak English as a second (or third or fourth) language. For a number of reasons, this population is the fastest growing in the United States. In both the 1970s and the 1980s, more immigrants were admitted to the United States than in any decade since the 1820s, with the slight exception of 1900-1910. In addition, during the 1970s and 1980s, some two million refugees were re-settled in the United States, and legislation (the Immigration Reform and Control Act of 1986) was passed making it possible for as many as two million more individuals residing in the country to apply for citizenship. The result of these events was a dramatic increase in the cultural and linguistic diversity of the United States population. Between the 1980 and 1990 censuses, the Hispanic population rose more than 50 percent, from 14.6 to 22.4 million, and the Asian-American population more than doubled, from 3.5 million to 7.3 million.

Although no one is certain about the degree of literacy, prior education, or English language proficiency of the immigrant and refugee population in the United States, of the 17 to 21 million individuals identified as "illiterate" by the English Language Proficiency Survey (ELPS) in 1982, 7 million were from homes where a language other than English was spoken (U.S. Department of Education, 1986; Wiley, 1991). A 1991 U.S. Department of Education report, *Teaching Adults with Limited English Skills: Progress and Challenges,* estimated that one third of those enrolled in adult literacy and adult basic education programs were enrolled in English as a second language (ESL) classes.

In any event, it is clear that there are large numbers of individuals with little or no prior education in their home countries who desire both English language and English literacy skills to permit them access to enhanced educational, social, political, and employment opportunities. Even those who have acquired literacy in their first language need to add English language and literacy skills to their repertoire. Those with substantial education and proficiency in English may still desire additional English language and literacy education, in addition to other training, to improve their employability or simply for personal growth and development.

The changing nature of the American workplace has also contributed to heightened attention to adult literacy (Crandall, in press). Computerization and increased employee responsibility in decision making (through quality circles and total quality management) have resulted in dramatic changes in employers' expectations of their employees. The assembly line of the past is being transformed by computerization and statistical process control into a place where workers must analyze and interpret a variety of numerical and graphic displays in order to make decisions about the quality of the product and the need for any changes. Likewise, clerical jobs that were once performed by several individuals may now be the responsibility of one individual with access to large databases through a networked computer. To meet these increased workplace expectations, a growing number of workplace literacy and education programs are being offered. Many of these programs focus on the needs of workers for whom English is a second language. In addition, a number of national studies have identified the need for potential changes in educating individuals for the "workplace of tomorrow," an issue made especially salient by the growing numbers of language minority individuals who will be part of the new workforce (Carnevale, Gainer, & Meltzer, 1990; Johnston & Packer, 1987). Success in the endeavor to better educate the workforce would encourage the development of more high-productivity/high-wage jobs, with increased responsibility placed on individual workers, according to one major study conducted by the Commission on the Skills of the American Workforce (1990). Failure would lead to an increase in low-wage employment, where previously complex jobs need to be simplified, and the work is less challenging.

Another factor creating renewed interest in adult literacy is the recognition of the role of parental literacy in children's school achievement, especially important in multilingual families where children have the added need of acquiring a second language (Weinstein-Shr, 1990). A review of early childhood education programs such as Head Start found that although these programs had an impact on children's educational achievement, the impact was short-lived. Greater impact and more lasting positive effects were created by parental education. The study found that the single most important factor in the academic achievement of children is the education of the mother (Sticht & McDonald, 1989). To break what has been referred to as the "cycle of illiteracy," a number of family literacy programs have been developed, providing adults with literacy instruction and other education aimed at helping them to achieve their own potential and to assist in their children's education. For language minority adults, this usually involves ESL literacy, among other program options.

Purposes for Literacy and Program Design

There are a number of reasons why adults participate in English language and literacy programs: to obtain or improve their employment; to continue their often disrupted education, obtaining a General Educational Development (GED) diploma as a first step; to be able to read to their children or assist them with their homework; to be able to write to family or friends left behind or to record their cultural traditions and stories for their children; or to improve their general situation and obtain some control or power over their lives.

To meet these different goals, a variety of programs have been developed. They include basic educational programs focusing on initial literacy or the development of more advanced reading and writing skills; family literacy programs focusing on ways in which parents and other caregivers can assist in the language and literacy development of their children; workplace literacy or worker education programs focusing on literacy, computation, decision making, and other skills needed to get or keep a job in the changing workplace or to improve employment options; and increasingly, programs that enable adults to engage in literacy and language learning for personal or community enrichment.

While these different program models exist, they have converged to a surprising degree in their instructional focus, attempting to accommodate the needs of the individual within the immediate context of the school or workplace, as well as providing an opportunity for community members to articulate and focus attention on particular goals, such as improving the general economic and social conditions in the community. Whether the approach is organized in terms of competencies and performance goals or more broadly in sociopolitical terms such as "empowerment," the emphasis is increasingly on meaningful, holistic, learner-centered instruction with learners involved in all stages of instruction, from program planning to evaluation. Even when a standardized test score is required by a program's funding source or outside evaluator, many programs also try to articulate goals and measure multiple outcomes in ways that are relevant and meaningful to the individual learner.

The majority of educational programs for adults who speak English as a second language involve both English language and literacy instruction. The need to teach both ESL and literacy has long been a challenge for adult educators in general and adult ESL educators in particular. Most programs have been designed for individuals who already are literate to some extent, and most adult instructors have rather limited experience in teaching both literacy and ESL. (See Foster, 1990, for further discussion.) What complicates the situation even more is the diversity of the population of learners and their languages and educational backgrounds. Some, such as the Hmong and Haitians, are members of predominantly oral cultures, with literacy confined to an elite who acquired it in another language, such as Lao or Thai (for the Hmong) or French (for the Haitians). Some come from cultures with a substantial literate tradition but have had few or no educational opportunities to acquire literacy. Even those with prior literacy may find that the transfer from a character-based or non-Roman-alphabet language to Roman-alphabet English represents a challenge to both learner and instructor.

Purpose of This Volume

One of the first tasks of the National Clearinghouse on Literacy Education (NCLE), which opened in September 1989 at the Center for Applied Linguistics, was to survey the field of adult literacy education for limited-English-proficient adults to ascertain the greatest needs for information and technical assistance. A recurrent theme in the responses from educators and program developers across the country was the need for a book summarizing the kinds of instructional approaches that can be used successfully with adults of limited English proficiency, with samples of the activities, strategies, or techniques that each approach might involve. The approaches mentioned included competency-based education; whole language, language experience, and Freirean or participatory approaches; and writing-based programs that result in published materials to be read by other adults. In reality, programs often combine several of these approaches. Even those programs that have adopted a competency-based approach—which may be perceived as quite different from the other, more holistic approaches—often incorporate language experience and process writing in their classes; likewise, more holistic or participatory programs may incorporate task-based learning in their classes. The differences are likely to reside in the basic philosophies upon which programs are designed and the degree to which the learners are engaged in overall direction setting. These five approaches represent the range of practice in ESL literacy instruction. Experts in these different approaches were commissioned to write papers for this volume.

The book's emphasis is on functional and holistic approaches to ESL literacy; there are no chapters dealing specifically with phonics. This should not be construed as a rejection of phonics, for attention to phonics is part of most adult literacy instructional programs. However, consistent with adult learning theory (Knowles, 1980), adult second language acquisition theory (Krashen, 1985), current reading theory (Smith, 1988), and second language reading theory in particular (Carrell, Devine, & Eskey, 1988), phonics is not the core of these programs. Adult education, following the theories of andragogy, stresses the importance of respecting and drawing upon the adult's experiences and providing instructional activities that reflect the cognitive and social development of each adult (Knowles, 1980), rather than requiring adults to wait until they have mastered the names of the letters, the correspondences between letters and sounds, and some words in isolation before they are presented with meaningful content. Second language acquisition theory and pedagogy also suggest that adults are best able to acquire a second language when they are provided with comprehensible and meaningful input, where the focus is not on the form (letters, spelling, or grammar) but on the content of the message (Krashen, 1982).

Moreover, as Krashen (1985) has pointed out, reading is a powerful source of input in acquiring a second language, a source that learners can carry with them outside class to continue acquisition even when they are alone. Thus, it is difficult to justify a delay in presenting meaningful reading passages to adults whose time for education is severely limited by their other responsibilities and focus, instead, on phonics for the crucial initial periods of instruction. (Few adults spend even 100 hours in adult literacy classes; most drop out during the first few weeks, making the initial weeks of any program of great importance.) The special features of English also argue against focusing initially on phonics. In English, spelling appears almost haphazard to all but the linguist, with so many letters or combinations of letters used to represent the same sounds; a focus on these correspondences in the initial stages may only frustrate the learner more.

Finally, current reading theory has increasingly questioned the use of *bottom up* approaches, which require learners to acquire literacy in a linear, additive fashion—from letters to words to phrases and sentences and finally to paragraphs and texts. Instead, the emphasis has shifted to interactive *(top down)* approaches, where meaningful text is presented from the outset, and smaller items such as letter-sound correspondences, vocabulary, or grammar are introduced as they become relevant. (See Carrell in Carrell, Devine, & Eskey, 1988, for further discussion.) When viewed from the many contexts and purposes of literacy instruction, where reading and writing are joined by oral communication, mathematics, problem solving, and decision making, it is easy to see how holistic, functional approaches have become dominant.

What about native language literacy and biliteracy (being literate in one's native language and in English)? This issue is more complicated. There is general agreement among linguists and educators about the importance of learning to read in one's first language: Most of one's prior cognitive and social development has occurred in the first language, making it easier to provide additional, literacy-related education in that language. However, a number of other factors have led to a preponderance of ESL literacy programs that focus primarily on the acquisition of English literacy with a much smaller emphasis on first language or biliteracy instruction. Among these factors is the diverse nature of the adult literacy population; where native language or biliteracy programs have been developed, there is usually a substantial community that speaks the same language. For example, some community-based initial or family literacy programs have enough speakers of the same language to be able to focus on literacy instruction in that language, but this is rarer in workplace literacy or worker education programs, where many different languages are usually represented.

A second factor influencing the availability of native language or biliteracy instruction is individual choice and the perceived benefits of English language literacy. Many adults, with very limited time for education, choose to spend that time in ESL literacy classes, focusing on citizenship, continued education, employment, or other immediate goals. They may add first language literacy later, but economic and educational pressures often encourage participation in ESL literacy instruction or at least discourage participation in first language literacy programs. In fact, many ESL literacy programs offer some degree of native language or biliteracy instruction as part of their program. What that instruction looks like, how it is implemented, when it occurs, and other factors that influence program design were the focus of a survey undertaken by NCLE. (Funding was provided through the National Center on Adult Literacy at the University of Pennsylvania, under a contract from the Office of Educational Research and Improvement, U.S. Department of Education.) To date, NCLE has collected information about approximately 60 programs that offer mother-tongue literacy instruction or some combination of mother-tongue and ESL literacy instruction, and maintains an up-to-date database of those programs. In addition, a collection of papers on theoretical and practical considerations in biliteracy (Spener, in press) has been prepared by NCLE staff.

Five Approaches to Adult ESL Literacy

The chapters in this volume present five approaches to adult ESL literacy: competency-based instruction, whole language, language experience, writing and publishing, and Freirean or participatory approaches. Although most adult literacy programs use strategies or techniques from several approaches, these five approaches represent the range of starting points within adult ESL literacy instruction, often reflecting the philosophy of the program as well as the relationships among learners, teachers, and instructional activities. The author of each chapter has many years of experience working within the particular approach and thus is able to provide not only a historical overview and introduction to the approach, but also a description of how the approach is implemented and some sample instructional strategies or activities that can be used.

The first chapter, "Literacy Through a Competency-Based Educational Approach," by K. Lynn Savage, provides an overview of what has been the most widely used approach in adult ESL and literacy for nearly two decades. In 1975, the Adult Performance Level project identified a set of competencies—the knowledge and the skills—viewed by some as basic for adults to function in the United States (Adult Performance Level Project Staff, 1975). Competency-based English language education has been the basis for the language and orientation programs in most refugee programs overseas and in the United States; it has also been an important influence in the development of adult language training programs in the U.S. Peace Corps. Moreover, a competency-based assessment system—the Comprehensive Adult Student Assessment System (CASAS)—is increasingly used to satisfy funders' requirements for adult literacy program evaluation. With its roots in functional literacy, competency-based education has come under recent attack. A number of theorists and practitioners have raised questions about the focus of competency-based education, particularly about who should design adult literacy programs and whose needs should be addressed. It is ironic that competency-based education has been criticized for not being sufficiently learner centered, because when it was introduced in the 1970s, it was heralded as an approach that focused specifically on learner needs. When learners participate in analyzing needs, setting objectives, and providing ongoing feedback about the direction of the program, competency-based programs can be learner centered. Today the competency-based approach is often adapted to reflect the particular sociocultural situation and needs of the specific learners through greater emphasis on both an initial needs assessment and ongoing evaluation by participants and program staff throughout the course of the program.

Savage brings a long history of involvement with competency-based education to this article. She has designed competency-based adult ESL educational programs for a variety of contexts, has taught within them, and has been responsible for a statewide adult teacher training program for competency-based education, which has been adopted by a number of other adult education programs and state departments of education across the country (Savage, 1984, 1991; Savage, Howe, & Yeung, 1982). In this chapter, she reviews the history, theory, and implementation of competency-based education. She then provides examples of the ways in which competency-based ESL literacy approaches can be used to teach prose literacy, document literacy, and quantitative literacy—the three types of literacy identified for testing by the National Assessment for Educational Progress (Kirsch & Jungeblut, 1986) that also serve as the basis for the 1992 National Adult Literacy Survey (see Macías, in press). Her review covers both academic and workplace literacy programs; both are contexts in which a competency-based approach to literacy instruction is commonly found.

Chapter Two, "Whole Language in Adult Literacy," by Pat Rigg and Francis E. Kazemek, presents the other major approach to adult ESL literacy instruction in the United States, one that is widely used in basic and family literacy programs and is also being tried with success in some workplace literacy programs (Crandall & Pharness, 1991). Rigg and Kazemek have written extensively on the need for adult literacy programs to be responsive to both individual and community needs and to provide participatory literacy instruction that assists adults in taking more control over their lives. They have also discussed ways in which a whole language philosophy or approach can accomplish these goals (Kazemek, 1985, 1988; Rigg, 1985, 1990; Rigg & Kazemek, 1985). In this chapter, they attempt to define whole language—a difficult, if not impossible task. As they put it, whole language is "not a method, nor is it a collection of strategies, techniques, or materials"; it is both "a view of language and of teaching and learning" and "a philosophy of education." Following that discussion, they describe whole language classrooms and a number of strategies or techniques that are used, including process-based writing. They conclude by describing model whole language programs, focusing special attention on the adult literacy and education program at the Invergarry Learning Centre in Surrey, British Columbia. At Invergarry, adults are engaged in writing of all types, some of which is published in a magazine of student writings, *Voices*, which is now widely distributed to other adult literacy programs. (The use of student writings as readings for adult literacy students is described more fully in Chapter Four.) It is mildly ironic (but also appropriate, because whole language is so difficult to define) that Invergarry does not use the term "whole language" to describe its own approach.

In the third chapter, "The Language Experience Approach," Marcia L. Taylor describes an approach that has been used effectively by both competency-based and whole language programs for decades and has become even more widely used today in initial, family, and even workplace ESL literacy programs. As they have done with whole language, educators in ESL literacy programs have borrowed language experience activities from the field of elementary and secondary school language arts education for native English speakers.

Taylor begins with a brief history of the approach, aligning it with whole language (of which it has become a common component) and contrasting it with phonics-based approaches. A discussion of how to use the language experience approach in both tutorial and larger group sessions follows. The discussion of tutorials adds an important dimension to this collection; many adult literacy programs involve one-on-one tutoring, often by an English monolingual tutor who may have little prior experience or training working with ethnolinguistically diverse students. Taylor closes by listing some possible topics for adult ESL literacy instructors to use as the basis for their language experience stories.

In Chapter Four, "Listening to Students' Voices: Publishing Students' Writing for Other Students to Read," Joy Kreeft Peyton describes what has become an exciting component, or often the core, of adult literacy programs: learner stories. Previously, a major problem facing adult ESL literacy programs was the lack of authentic reading materials at the appropriate level of English language proficiency that were also of interest to new readers. Now, increasing numbers of adult literacy instructors, both for ESL and mother tongue literacy, are encouraging adult learners to write about their experiences and then publishing these writings, either singly or in collections, and making them available for other adult learners to read. This strategy is also used in many whole language programs, including those mentioned in Rigg and Kazemek's chapter. Using process-based writing or the writing workshop as a basis of instruction, instructors have not only been able to provide meaningful, relevant literacy instruction for adult ESL learners, but they have also been able to produce a vast array of interesting literature for other new learners to read.

Calling upon her broad experience with the teaching of writing (Peyton, 1990; Peyton & Staton, 1991; Peyton, Staton, Richardson, & Wolfram, 1990), Peyton reviews the benefits of a writing-centered ESL literacy program and describes the steps involved in the writing process. She concludes with sources of publications by new writers for new readers.

"The Freirean Approach to Adult Literacy Education," by David Spener, explains both the theoretical background to liberatory education and the ways it has been and can be implemented in the ESL literacy classroom. Spener's close study of Paolo Freire's and his own use of participatory literacy practices in his ESL literacy teaching have provided him with an excellent perspective from which to describe the feasibility of implementing these practices in educational settings in the United States. (See Spener, 1990, for further discussion.) In reality, Freire provides more of a philosophy of education than a set of techniques or strategies, although dialogue and problem posing are usually included as means of focusing and organizing instruction. After discussing both dialogue and problem posing, Spener provides examples of ways these techniques can be adapted for the ESL literacy classroom, drawing on his experience in teaching adult ESL in the *Inglés en su Casa* program. He ends with a discussion of "theoretical critiques and pragmatic considerations" of Freirean literacy education occasioned by the attempts to apply Freire's philosophy to urban ESL and native language literacy programs that reflect the more recent views of literacy as social practice.

These five chapters provide a window on adult ESL literacy instruction in the United States and reflect the variety of effective practices and programs that are available. In addition to discussing the theoretical underpinnings of each approach, the authors draw on their practical experiences to provide adult literacy program administrators and instructors with guidance on implementing the approach in their programs. That many of these same approaches can, and are, used in mother tongue or biliteracy programs makes the volume even more comprehensive.

References

Adult Performance Level Project Staff. (1975). *Adult functional competency: A summary*. Austin, TX: University of Texas. (ERIC Document Reproduction Service No. ED 114 609)

Carnevale, A.P., Gainer, L.J., & Meltzer, A.S. (1990). *Workplace basics: The essential skills employers want*. San Francisco: Jossey-Bass.

Carrell, P., Devine, J., & Eskey, D. (1988). *Interactive approaches to second language reading*. Cambridge: Cambridge University Press.

Chisman, F.P., & Associates (Eds.). (1990). *Leadership for literacy: The agenda for the 1990s*. San Francisco: Jossey-Bass.

Commission on the Skills of the American Workforce. (1990). *America's choice: High skills or low wages*. Rochester, NY: National Center on Education and the Economy.

Crandall, J.A. (in press). Language, literacy and multiculturalism. In C. Kreidler (Ed.), *Proceedings of the 1991 Georgetown University Roundtable on Languages and Linguistics*. Washington, DC: Georgetown University Press.

Crandall, J.A., & Pharness, G. (1991). Whole language approaches in adult literacy. In C. Monnastes (Ed.), *Launching the literacy decade: Awareness into action* (pp. 141-151). Banff, Alberta, Canada: International Reading Association/Multiculturalism and Citizenship Bureau of Canada.

Foster, S.E. (1990). Upgrading the skills of literacy professionals: The profession matures. In F.P. Chisman & Associates (Eds.), *Leadership for literacy: The agenda for the 1990s* (pp. 73-95). San Francisco: Jossey-Bass.

Johnston, W.B., & Packer, A.H. (1987). *Workforce 2000: Work and workers for the 21st century*. Indianapolis: Hudson Institute. (ERIC Document Reproduction Service No. ED 290 887)

Kazemek, F.E. (1985). An examination of the Adult Performance Level Project and its effects upon adult literacy education in the United States. *Lifelong Learning, 9*, 4-8.

Kazemek, F.E. (1988). Necessary changes: Professional involvement in adult literacy programs. *Harvard Educational Review, 58*, 464-487.

Kirsch, I.S., & Jungeblut, A. (1986). *Literacy: Profiles of America's young adults*. Princeton, NJ: Educational Testing Service, National Assessment of Educational Progress.

Knowles, M.S. (1980). *The modern practice of adult education: From pedagogy to andragogy*. Chicago: Associated Press/Follett.

Krashen, S.D. (1982). *Principles and practice in second language acquisition*. Oxford: Pergamon.

Krashen, S.D. (1985). *Inquiries & insights*. Hayward, CA: Alemany.

Macías, R.F. (in press). Inheriting sins while seeking absolution: English literacy, biliteracy, language diversity, and national data sets. In D. Spener (Ed.), *Adult biliteracy in the United States*. McHenry, IL and Washington, DC: Delta Systems and Center for Applied Linguistics.

Peyton, J.K. (1990). *Listening to students' voices: Educational materials written by and for adults learning English*. Washington, DC: Center for Applied Linguistics, National Clearinghouse on Literacy Education. (ERIC Document Reproduction Service No. ED 317 096)

Peyton, J.K., & Staton, J. (1991). *Writing our lives: Reflections on dialogue journal writing with adults learning English*. Englewood Cliffs, NJ: Regents Prentice Hall/Center for Applied Linguistics.

Peyton, J.K., Staton, J., Richardson, G., & Wolfram, W. (1990). The influence of writing task on ESL students' written production. *Research in the Teaching of English, 24*(2), 142-171.

Rigg, P. (1985). Petra, learning to read at 45. *Journal of Education, 167*, 129-139.

Rigg, P. (1990). Whole language in adult ESL programs. *ERIC/CLL News Bulletin, 13*(2), 1, 4-6.

Rigg, P., & Kazemek, F.E. (1985). For adults only: Reading materials for adult literacy students. *Journal of Reading, 28*, 726-731.

Savage, K.L. (1984, January). *Teaching strategies for developing literacy skills in non-native speakers of English*. Paper presented at the National Adult Literacy Conference, Washington, DC. (ERIC Document Reproduction Service No. ED 240 296)

Savage, K.L. (Producer). (1991). *Teacher training through video: CBE and ESL techniques* [Video]. White Plains, NY: Longman.

Savage, K.L., Howe, M., & Yeung, E.L. (1982). *English that works*. Glenview, IL: Scott, Foresman.

Smith, F. (1988). *Understanding reading*. Hillsdale, NJ: Lawrence Erlbaum.

Spener, D. (1990). *The Freirean approach to adult literacy education*. Washington, DC: Center for Applied Linguistics, National Clearinghouse on Literacy Education. (ERIC Document Reproduction Service No. ED 321 615)

Spener, D. (in press). *Adult biliteracy in the United States*. McHenry, IL and Washington, DC: Delta Systems and Center for Applied Linguistics.

Sticht, T.G., & McDonald, B.A. (1989). *Making the nation smarter: The intergenerational transfer of cognitive ability*. San Diego: Institute for the Study of Adult Literacy.

U.S. Department of Education. (1986). *Adult literacy initiative: Update on adult illiteracy fact sheet*. Washington, DC: U.S. Government Printing Office.

U.S. Department of Education. (1991). *Teaching adults with limited English skills: Progresses and challenges*. Washington, DC: Author.

Weinstein-Shr, G. (1990). *Family and intergenerational literacy in multilingual families*. Washington, DC: Center for Applied Linguistics, National Clearinghouse on Literacy Education. (ERIC Document Service No. 321 624)

Wiley, T. (1991). *Measuring the nation's literacy: Important considerations*. Washington, DC: Center for Applied Linguistics, National Clearinghouse on Literacy Education. (ERIC Document Reproduction Service No. ED 334 868)

CHAPTER 1
Literacy Through a Competency-Based Educational Approach

K. Lynn Savage
California Department of Education,
Adult Education Unit

This chapter describes competency-based education (CBE) as one approach to literacy instruction in English as a second language (ESL). It provides the reader with a CBE definition, historical perspective, and syllabus design. It presents literacy instruction in competency-based ESL programs from the perspective of two distinctly different types of learner goals: survival and academic. For survival literacy, it provides examples of instructional materials and activities that teach document literacy, quantitative literacy, and prose literacy. For academic literacy, this chapter distinguishes between objectives and strategies for those who have limited literacy in their first language and for those who have first language literacy skills and intermediate-level English proficiency, both oral and written.

Competency-Based Education

Competency-based education (CBE) is a functional approach to education that emphasizes life skills and evaluates mastery of those skills according to actual learner performance. It was defined by the U. S. Office of Education as "a performance-based process leading to demonstrated mastery of basic and life skills necessary for the individual to function proficiently in society" (U.S. Office of Education, 1978).

In the narrowest sense, "life skills" have been interpreted to mean basic survival skills, such as those needed to answer personal information questions, to use public transportation, or to obtain food and shelter. In a broader sense, life skills have been interpreted to include all of the skills needed to function in any situation in which language plays a role: taking notes during an academic lecture; following directions for a work-related task, such as tuning up a car, or for an academic task, such as conducting a laboratory experiment; explaining one's position on an issue; or distinguishing between fact and opinion in a newspaper editorial.

Controversy about the scope and usefulness of CBE (Auerbach, 1986; Auerbach & Burgess, 1985; Tollefson, 1989) may be the result of a narrow interpretation. The CBE approach is applicable to students with academic, employment, and self-enrichment goals as well as to those with "survival" goals. It is applicable to students with a high level of English proficiency as well as to those with limited or no English proficiency. It is applicable to students who have had a rich education in their own language or home country as well as to those who have had no education in their home country. It is also applicable to students whose cultures are similar to the U.S. culture as well as to those whose cultures provide a sharp contrast to the U.S. culture. Programs may choose to limit the range of competencies in their curriculum due to the student population they serve, but a limited range of competencies is not inherent in CBE.

In addition to interpreting CBE as an approach that limits the range of competencies developed, critics tend to confuse characteristics of specific programs with characteristics of CBE. For example, some programs attempting to implement CBE have developed a curriculum that uses a formulaic, phrase-book approach to teaching language. However, a CBE curriculum can do much more than that. With the use of a communicative syllabus, it can build student capacity to generate language. By using the techniques introduced by Paulo Freire's work on problem posing (see Spener, this volume), a CBE curriculum can stimulate students to use critical thinking and problem-solving skills. A CBE curriculum can develop the four language skills of listening, speaking, reading, and writing through a whole language approach. Programs may choose a particular approach to language teaching based on the philosophy of their instructional staff, but no one language teaching methodology is inherent in CBE.

CBE is, in fact, a process that can be applied to teaching any content area. The process is cyclical, involving four components: assessment of student needs, selection of competencies based on those needs, instruction targeted to those competencies, and evaluation of student performance in those competencies to determine if students have mastered the instructional content (California CBAE Staff Development Project, 1983; ESL Teacher Institute, 1990).

A competency is an instructional objective described in task-based terms. Sample competencies include following directions to a place, answering personal information questions, interpreting a bus schedule, and writing a check. Competency statements begin with "students will be able to . . . ." Verbs that complete the statement must be demonstrable, such as *answer, interpret, request*. Verbs such as *understand* and *know* are not demonstrable and do not identify tasks and are, therefore, unacceptable in competency statements. The competency statement guides the instructional plan. Evaluation is based on demonstrated performance of the competency.

Historical Perspective

CBE evolved from a study conducted by the Adult Performance Level (APL) Project at the University of Texas (APL Project Staff, 1975). The APL Project identified five areas of knowledge for an adult to possess in order to function successfully in today's society: occupational, consumer, health, government and law, and community resources. Also identified were skills needed to function in each area. The skills included listening and speaking, reading and writing, interpersonal relations, problem solving, and computation.

Initially, the impact of the APL study was on adult basic education programs in general. However, soon after the influx of Southeast Asian refugees, the APL study had a major impact on English as a second language instruction as well. A guide, *Teaching ESL to Competencies* (Language and Orientation Resource Center, 1982), was developed for refugee programs in the United States, and a list of minimal competencies, first developed in Oregon, was adapted for the refugee camps in Southeast Asia.

Ultimately, there were mandates from policy makers at state and national levels for a competency-based approach to adult education. These mandates resulted in the development of tests, manuals for implementing CBE programs, and training materials.

Tests. Two significant assessment instruments were developed: one by the Comprehensive Adult Student Assessment System (CASAS) consortium and the other by the Center for Applied Linguistics (CAL).

CASAS began in 1980 as a consortium of adult education agencies in California. Initially, the consortium identified competencies and developed and field tested life skills reading items related to those competencies. It has since developed listening items. Both the life skills reading and the listening items have been used to produce *Life Skills Survey Achievement Tests* (Comprehensive Adult Student Assessment System, 1982). The tests are available for purchase through CASAS provided the purchasing agency has received training in administering them.

The Center for Applied Linguistics was contracted in the early 1980s by the Office of Refugee Resettlement (of the U.S. Department of Health and Human Services) to design a test for newly arrived Southeast Asian refugees enrolled in adult education programs. The result, the *Basic English Skills Test* (BEST) (Center for Applied Linguistics, 1982), is a performance-based test of ESL survival skills that consists of two parts. In the core section, which is administered individually, the learner gives verbal or nonverbal responses to stimuli such as pictures and examiner's questions. In the literacy section, which can be administered individually or to a group, students respond by marking or writing.

Manuals. In order to assist agencies in implementing competency-based adult education (CBAE) in California, *The Handbook for CBAE Staff Development* (California CBAE, 1983) was produced. It provides chapters on management, assessment, guidance, and instruction as well as an overview of CBAE.

The *Competency-Based Mainstream English Language Training* (MELT) *Technical Assistance Resource Package* (Office of Refugee Resettlement, 1986) was developed to assist refugee programs across the country. The MELT consists of the following products: the Student Performance Levels, which describe students' language abilities at a given level in terms of listening, speaking, reading, and writing skills; the MELT Core Curriculum, which is to be used along with the performance levels; and the Basic English Skills Test (BEST), selected because it can discriminate language proficiency levels among beginning literates. These products provide a basis for the design and operation of programs involved in refugee language training. The package also includes activities and materials to conduct workshops for educators working with refugees. It was developed by a team representing five different states (all substantially affected by Southeast Asian refugees), field-tested across the country, and revised by the team.

Training Products. In order to provide training for instructors implementing CBE, both California and Virginia developed products for use by trainers. The Virginia product, *Competency-based Teacher Education Workshops in CBE/ESL* (Schaffer & Van Duzer, 1984), provides outlines and activities for a series of workshops. The California products, *Implementing CBAE in the ESL Classrooms: Beginning Level* and *Implementing CBAE in the ESL Classrooms: Intermediate Level* (CBAE Staff Development Project, 1986), provide trainers with relevant background information, a video that shows an ESL class using CBE instruction, and activities for use in training.

The CBE movement in adult education occurred at about the same time as the development of English for special purposes (ESP) in ESL programs, an approach to language learning that enables learners to cope with clearly defined tasks of practical use in achieving occupational and academic aims (Hutchinson & Waters, 1987; Widdowson, 1983). CBE and ESP share two underlying assumptions: Basic skills such as grammatical structures are a means to an end, not an end in themselves; and learning should be directly related to application.

Recent developments in English language instruction for ESL learners at the secondary level reflect an acceptance of these assumptions. These developments include "sheltered" English, an instructional approach used to make academic instruction in English understandable to students with limited English proficiency (Christian, Spanos, Crandall, Simich-Dudgeon, & Willets, 1990; Freeman & Freeman, 1988), and ESL in content areas, in which content material is incorporated into language classes (Brinton, Snow, & Wesche, 1989; California State Department of Education, 1990b; Crandall, 1987; Short, 1991).

Syllabus Design

The CBE syllabus is usually organized around topics. Often they are drawn from the five content areas identified in the APL study or from subtopics within those five areas. For example, the area of community resources may include the topics of transportation, post office, and recreation.

For each topic there may be several different objectives, each stated in terms of life skill competencies. From these life skill competencies, the instructor determines the basic skills (linguistic skills such as grammar, pronunciation, and conversation as well as listening, speaking, reading, writing, and computation) necessary for the life skill. Basic skills are not a goal in themselves but are important means by which students can achieve the life skill competency. Instruction first focuses on teaching the enabling skills in context and then on the application of the enabling skill to the life skill (California CBAE, 1983). For example, if the objective is to write a check (life skill), the learner must first be able to write money amounts in words and to write dates (enabling skills).

The major consideration in CBE syllabus design is the relevance of the competency to student needs. The instructor may determine needs in one of several different ways. Students may complete a written questionnaire or participate in an oral interview. The instructor might also predict needs based on knowledge of the students, such as educational level, age, residence, and length of time in the United States. Ideally, both approaches are used together to identify needed competencies, and needs are reassessed often throughout the program. If students do not need to perform a particular competency in English, then inclusion of that competency in the syllabus is not appropriate.

Needs assessments may be general or specific, with student goals determining courses as well as objectives within courses. Goals students identify may range from basic survival, vocational training, or employment to participation in academic programs such as adult basic education, citizenship, or community college credit classes.

Competency-Based ESL Literacy

Survival literacy is the most common, most immediate goal of literacy instruction in competency-based ESL programs. It is the ability to recognize and to produce in writing those English language items that are commonly required outside the classroom. A secondary, but longer term, goal is for students to use literacy as a tool for further learning, that is, to acquire academic literacy.

Survival Literacy

There are four types of students who may require instruction in survival literacy (Language and Orientation Resource Center, 1981; Savage, 1984). Adult ESL programs currently have a large number of students in each of these four categories.

1. *Preliterate.* Students speak a language for which there is not a written form or whose written form is rare (e.g., Hmong, Mien).

2. *Nonliterate*. Students speak a language for which there is a written form but do not read or write themselves.

3. *Semiliterate*. Students have some formal education or are able to read and write but only at an elementary level.

4. *Literate in a non-Roman alphabet language* (e.g., Arabic, Cambodian, Cantonese, Farsi, Korean, Thai). Students are literate in their first language but need to learn the formation of the Roman alphabet and the sound/symbol relationship of English.

In survival literacy, reading and writing instruction is closely related to the contexts in which learners need to read and write. Instruction focused on a topic such as shopping would require literacy instruction that enables students to recognize prices and read labels. Instruction focused on small-talk topics such as favorite foods, weekend activities, or the weather would not require literacy instruction.

The following is an example of a survival literacy lesson using a competency-based approach. The topic is personal identification. The listening and speaking instruction focuses on names (e.g., What is your first name, last name, middle initial, maiden name?) and numbers (e.g., What is your social security number, telephone number, alien registration number?). In a competency-based approach, the literacy objectives would be to recognize print found on forms (e.g., name, telephone number) and to produce information requested on forms (e.g., student's own name and own identification numbers).

Students who are preliterate or nonliterate require additional activities prior to working with forms. These additional activities might include the following:

- Matching pictures with words.
- Identifying words without visual clues, such as from a passage or from a vocabulary set.
- Matching words written on flashcards with a word in a passage written on the chalkboard.
- Selecting and arranging letters from a set of alphabet cards to form a word.
- Filling in letters that are missing in a word written on the chalkboard.
- Copying words.

Document literacy. Initially, the reading needs of most adult ESL learners involve *document literacies,* the skills and strategies required to locate and use information contained in tables, graphs, charts, indexes, forms, schedules, and other nontextual materials (Kirsch & Jungeblut, 1986). Document literacy can be categorized by three general types:

1. Tables or charts with rows and columns, found in bus schedules and telephone bills.
2. Tables with headings and boxes, found in payroll stubs and gas, electric, and water bills.
3. Text consisting of words or phrases such as those found on clothing care labels and in newspaper classified ads.

In teaching document literacy, instructors need to provide prereading activities that encourage students to bring their previous knowledge and experience to the reading. They need to provide guidance in the organizational structure of the reading and practice activities that reflect real-life tasks that would accompany such readings.

The following example is a lesson that focuses on reading clothing care labels like the one shown.

```
MACHINE WASH WARM
REGULAR CYCLE
TUMBLE DRY LOW
```

The instructor begins the lesson by asking students a series of questions such as the following:

1. How do you find out how to wash something? Where do you look?
2. Where is that label usually found?
3. What are two ways to wash your clothes?
4. What does the label tell you about washing?
5. What are some possible temperatures of the water?
6. The cycle is set according to the type of fabric being washed. What different cycles does a washing machine have?
7. What are different ways you can dry clothes?

Then the instructor writes on the chalkboard the information elicited, in categories such as the following:

Wash	Temp.	Cycle	Dry
hand	cool	gentle	flat
machine	cold	regular	hang
	hot	heavy-duty	tumble
	warm		

In real life, written items are not read from beginning to end, but rather scanned to find specific information. To give students practice, the instructor provides a worksheet such as the one below to complete for different clothing labels.

WASH _____

    temperature _____

    cycle _____

DRY _____

    temperature _____

    iron temperature _____

(from Savage, 1992a)

This worksheet design encourages scanning and does not require students to read from beginning to end. It uses key words, not complete sentences, and students write only the information requested, not complete sentences.

Quantitative literacy. Readers usually have specific reasons for reading a document. Therefore, in competency-based materials, an extension exercise that requires students to do something with the information they have read frequently follows comprehension activities. For example, an exercise on reading a train schedule might ask, "You need to be in Los Angeles by 3:00 p.m. Which train should you take?" An exercise on reading a payroll stub might ask, "What was the difference between gross and net pay?" An exercise on reading a telephone bill might ask, "What was the cost per minute for the three-minute telephone call to Chicago on July 22?" Questions such as these encourage the development of quantitative literacy, defined as "the knowledge and skills needed to apply arithmetic operations . . . that are embedded in printed materials, such as in balancing a checkbook . . . or completing an order form" (Kirsch & Jungeblut, 1986, p. 4).

Prose literacy. In addition to document and quantitative literacy, ESL learners may also need prose literacy, defined as "the knowledge and skills needed to understand and use information contained in various kinds of textual material" (Kirsch & Jungeblut, 1986, p. 8). Even though materials such as employee handbooks, health plan descriptions, credit card agreements, and rental agreements are presented in prose, competent readers are more likely to scan for specific information than to read from beginning to end. Activities to accompany readings to develop prose literacy include prereading, comprehension, and extension. Following the sample reading text (taken from a lesson on emergency procedures) are samples of prereading, comprehension, and extension activities that might accompany the reading.

FIRE

Fire is the third largest accidental killer in the nation. Over 80% of all deaths by fire occur where people sleep—in houses, apartments, or hotels. Fire is the disaster you and your family members are most likely to experience.

DANGERS AND PREVENTIVE MEASURES

One of the greatest dangers of fire is asphyxiation—death from lack of oxygen. To avoid asphyxiation when you are in a smoke-filled room, move by crawling on your hands and knees. The air will be the freshest about one foot above the floor. The hot air, with carbon monoxide and other poisonous gases, will rise.

Another danger of fire is failure to wake up. To avoid sleeping through a fire, you should install a smoke alarm on the wall or ceiling of each bedroom. A smoke alarm can warn you if a fire breaks out when you are sleeping. If there are any bedrooms on an upper level, you should also install a smoke alarm in the center of the ceiling above the stairway.

PREPARATION

To be prepared for a fire in your home, you need to know how to get out. You should plan with your family at least two ways to get out of every room in your home.

EQUIPMENT/SUPPLIES

One thing you should have on hand is a fire extinguisher. There are three types of fire extinguishers: Type A is for ordinary combustibles (paper, cloth, wood, rubber, many plastics); Type B is for flammable liquids (oils, gasoline, kitchen greases, paints, solvents); Type C is for electrical fires (in wiring, fuse boxes, motors, power tools, appliances). If you have only one fire extinguisher, it should be a multi-purpose type labeled A-B-C, which puts out most types of fires.

You should also keep baking soda near the stove in your kitchen. Baking soda is especially effective for smothering cooking fires.

From *Building Life Skills 3,* by K. L. Savage, 1989, p. 5, White Plains, NY: Longman. Reprinted by permission.

Prereading questions help students identify the kinds of information that might be found in the reading. Sample questions follow:

1. Are fires common in your country?
2. Were you ever in a fire?
3. What did you do to be prepared?
4. Have you heard about any fires in this country?
5. What happened?
6. Do you know what to do to be prepared?

Comprehension exercises encourage students to scan for specific information in the text. The following questions might accompany the text on emergency procedures:

1. What kind of disaster is presented in the reading?
2. What is one danger in this kind of disaster?
3. What is another danger?
4. What can you do to avoid these dangers?
5. What do you need to know in order to be prepared?
6. What are some things you should have on hand?

Extension exercises require students to do something with the information they get. Questions such as the following might be used to personalize and extend the emergency procedures reading.

1. How many rooms are there where you live? Are there two ways you could get out of each room?
2. Do you have any smoke alarms? If so, where are they installed?
3. Do you have a fire extinguisher? If so, do you know how to use it?

ESL learners may also need to read prose from beginning to end, such as in a note from a supervisor or fellow employee, a letter from a child's school, or an article in a company publication. Exercises most appropriate to the real-life demand of such readings are ones that require restating, paraphrasing, or summarizing.

In summary, survival literacy as described above relates reading and writing instruction to what is required to meet basic life skill objectives. In the unit on personal information, literacy instruction focused on reading and completing forms. In the unit on clothing labels, literacy instruction focused on scanning print for specific vocabulary related to directions for cleaning and producing print to demonstrate comprehension. In the unit on emergency procedures, literacy instruction focused on scanning for specific information and using that information to draw important conclusions.

Academic Literacy

CBE programs are not limited to developing survival skills alone. A second and equally important literacy need of many ESL learners that can be met by a CBE approach is the development of reading and writing skills for academic purposes. Two distinct types of literacy instruction are included in this category. Instruction for students who bring with them literacy skills in their first language and some English language proficiency is referred to below as English for academic purposes (EAP). Instruction that provides a transition between survival literacy and EAP is required for students who have limited literacy skills in their first language. This transitional phase is referred to below as literacy for learning.

Literacy for learning. Not all learners with academic goals have literacy skills in their first language, so they may initially be unable to progress in academic settings. Developing literacy for learning— for example, reading to review text and aid memory (see Savage & Mrowicki, 1990) or writing to take notes on information presented or read—is essential for less literate adult immigrant learners if they are to succeed in mainstream programs such as adult basic education, high school equivalency, vocational training, and community college credit classes, as well as advanced-level ESL classes.

Literacy activities at this transitional level focus on developing students' ability to read and write language already encountered through listening and speaking. The content must be relevant to the students; that is, content arises from student interest, personal experience, or needs. Oral work precedes reading and writing (Blanton, 1990; Savage, 1984; see also Peyton, Taylor, this volume). The content may be presented in the form of a dialogue or a language experience story. In either case, the instructor presents the content and provides oral practice before beginning the literacy portion of the lesson. Next, the instructor presents learners with the print version of the language, which is then used to develop reading skills.

When language experience lessons are used, the instructor must first create a common experience for the class. Field trips and in-class activities can create a common experience. One example of in-class activities that lend themselves to the language experience approach is demonstrations by the instructor of steps in a process. The demonstration may be as simple as making coffee, tea, or hot chocolate, or it may be more complex, such as following a recipe. (See Taylor, this volume, for a more detailed discussion of the language experience approach.)

Language experience lessons revolving around steps in a process begin with listening; students watch the instructor do something and listen to the instructor describe each step in the process. This teacher-centered activity then becomes student-centered when the students follow directions to produce the hot chocolate, for example. After students are familiar with the process and the language used to describe the process, the instructor elicits a story from them and writes it on the chalkboard.

The story that has been elicited is used to develop reading skills. The following activities may be included:

- Matching a word card to a duplicate word in a sentence in the story.
- Reading words from the story in isolation on word cards.
- Reading a sentence from the story orally (without word cards).
- Arranging word cards into a sentence.
- Reading a sentence made up of word cards.
- Arranging sentence strips into a story.
- Reading the entire story without help.

(Savage, 1984)

The story can also be used to develop writing skills. For a lesson on following a recipe, the instructor may have students list ingredients as well as each step in the process.

In a competency-based approach, the literacy objective for a language experience lesson revolving around the steps in a process would be to follow the written directions (such as on a recipe card, a jar of instant coffee or cocoa, or pre-packaged food boxes). Activities to develop reading skills focus not only on the sentence level but also on the relationship between sentences. Students read each step of the process and relate steps to each other. Instructors may have students identify what comes before and after specific steps or have them sequence sentence strips. Developing the skills of sequencing and identifying relationships enables students to follow written directions in a specific multiple-step task. The skills needed to complete this task can be transferred to other multiple-step tasks, such as purchasing stamps from a postage machine, using a pay telephone, changing engine oil, or sending a fax. These language experience activities are transferable because they are concrete, which is appropriate for students who have no more than survival literacy skills; and they result in extended text, which is common in academic reading materials.

English for academic purposes. For students at an intermediate level of oral and written English proficiency who have academic goals, English for academic purposes (EAP) is appropriate. EAP is especially relevant to students who come from cultures in which expectations for academic success are significantly different from the expectations in the United States.

Literacy activities at this level differ from literacy for learning in two ways: Passages are longer than one paragraph, and frequently several passages are presented at once; and the written information is new to the students—listening and speaking activities do not precede the reading. Students are expected to get new information from readings and to present new information in writing.

Competencies necessary for academic success include selecting relevant information from lectures, taking lecture notes, summarizing or paraphrasing readings, skimming for main ideas, scanning for specific information, recalling facts and ideas, interpreting tables and other illustrations that accompany text, and predicting outcomes (California State Department of Education, 1990a; Chamot & O'Malley, 1987).

The following is an example of a lesson that focuses on English for academic purposes. The topic is two great presidents, George Washington and Abraham Lincoln (see Savage, 1992b, for the reading). Students are expected to recall facts about the lives of Lincoln and Washington, to compare their lives, and to identify someone of equal historical significance in their own country.

The instructor begins the lesson by focusing students' attention on pictures of Lincoln and Washington. Eliciting information students already know about each president, the instructor writes the information on the chalkboard. After receiving a copy of the story, students discuss the topic of presidents (possibly of their own countries) before reading the text silently. These prereading activities encourage students to bring their knowledge and experience to the reading. They also reinforce the use of skimming for content highlights.

The instructor provides the students several opportunities to read the story—once to themselves, once while the instructor reads aloud, once to circle words that are new—before checking comprehension. Finally, in order to develop students' reading skills, the instructor has students do the following: categorize by dividing sentences into two groups, one about Washington and one about Lincoln; sequence the sentences within each category; complete a cloze passage; complete a vocabulary exercise, matching words with meanings; and answer comprehension questions that include factual and interpretation questions, such as, "Who is the most famous president in the history of your country?" or "What do people in your country consider to be important qualities of a good president?" (Savage, 1992b).

The reading can also be used to develop writing skills. The instructor may have students use a timeline to indicate significant events in each of the figure's lives, develop a timeline for significant events in the life of a leader from their own country, write a paragraph that describes the significant events in another person's life, or write a theme that compares two other leaders.

This lesson enables students to identify facts about Washington and Lincoln, two individuals of significance in U.S. history. It develops familiarity with two different ways of organizing prose—chronological order and comparison and contrast. The strategies used to indicate chronology are transferable to other historical events as well as to biographical information about other historically significant people.

The strategies used to compare and contrast are transferable to other topics as well, such as cities (compare the town of your birth with your current home town), landmarks (compare a famous building in your native country with a famous building in this country), and geography (compare the physical characteristics of your native state or province with those of the state of your current residence).

In summary, CBE programs may include academic literacy as well as survival literacy. Students who have academic goals may have limited literacy skills in their first language, or they may be literate in their first language. If students wish to pursue further study for vocational, academic, or personal enrichment, literacy instruction for academic purposes is important, as instruction in these courses usually requires students both to read and to produce materials that are in English.

Academic literacy for less literate students involves literacy for learning. The instructor develops reading activities from the print version of materials in which students have previously had oral practice. The reading activities focus on sentences and relationships among sentences within a passage. Follow-up activities may encourage writing to recall key elements of the reading passage.

Academic literacy for students with intermediate-level English proficiency is called English for academic purposes. The instructor presents reading passages that provide students with new information and uses the passages to develop reading skills such as skimming, scanning, and interpreting. Follow-up activities may require students to produce paragraphs or papers that reflect the organizational structure used in the passage and that are similar to those required in an academic program.

Conclusion

In ESL programs that are competency-based, students may need literacy instruction for survival or for academic purposes. Survival literacy identifies specific items within the language that must be recognized in print or produced in writing for basic survival purposes outside the classroom. It distinguishes between reading (recognition items) and writing (production items). Students are not expected to write language that they will only need to recognize in the real world.

Academic literacy includes literacy for learning, which provides a transition between survival literacy and English for academic purposes. This stage is necessary for students who have limited literacy skills in their first language. It is not necessary for students who already have first language literacy skills and some English language proficiency. In literacy for learning, reading activities are derived from dialogues and language experience stories. Activities focus on reading sentences and on relationships among sentences, as well as on word recognition.

When students have skills recognizing and producing print from their own life experiences, instruction proceeds to getting new information from print. Both document literacies and extended printed prose are appropriate. To introduce prose, the instructor uses simplified reading passages of more than one paragraph. Activities focus on the organization and relationship within and among paragraphs as well as on comprehension and interpretation. Finally, the instructor introduces authentic texts, continuing to provide activities that focus on organization, comprehension, and interpretation.

ESL literacy instruction, whether survival or academic, is competency-based if the needs of the students have been assessed, the competencies have been selected based on those needs, the instruction is targeted to those competencies, and the students are evaluated based on performance of those competencies.

References

Adult Performance Level Project Staff. (1975). *Adult functional competency: A summary*. Austin, TX: University of Texas. (ERIC Document Reproduction Service No. ED 114 609)

Auerbach, E.R. (1986) Competency-based ESL: One step forward or two steps back? *TESOL Quarterly*, *20*, 411-429.

Auerbach, E.R., & Burgess, D. (1985). The hidden curriculum of survival ESL. *TESOL Quarterly*, *19*, 475-495.

Blanton, L. (1990). *Talking adult ESL students into writing: Building on oral fluency to promote literacy*. Washington, DC: Center for Applied Linguistics, National Clearinghouse on Literacy Education. (ERIC Document Reproduction Service No. ED 321 622)

Brinton, D.M., Snow, M.A., & Wesche, G. (1989). *Content-based second language instruction*. New York: Newbury House.

California CBAE Staff Development Project. (1983). *Handbook for CBAE staff development*. San Francisco: San Francisco State University, Center for Adult Education.

California CBAE Staff Development Project. (1986a). *Implementing CBAE in the ESL classroom: Beginning level*. LaPuente, CA: Outreach and Technical Assistance Network.

California CBAE Staff Development Project. (1986b). *Implementing CBAE in the ESL classroom: Intermediate level*. LaPuente, CA: Outreach and Technical Assistance Network.

California State Department of Education. (1990a). *Bilingual education handbook: Designing instruction for LEP students*. Sacramento, CA: Author.

California State Department of Education. (1990b). *English as a second language handbook for adult education instructors*. Sacramento, CA: Author.

Center for Applied Linguistics. (1982). *Basic English Skills Test*. Washington, DC: Author.

Chamot, A.U., & O'Malley, J.M. (1987). The cognitive academic learning approach: A bridge to the mainstream. *TESOL Quarterly, 21*, 227-250.

Christian, D., Spanos, G., Crandall, J., Simich-Dudgeon, C., & Willets, K. (1990). Combining language and content for second-language students. In A.M. Padilla, H.H. Fairchild, & C.M. Valadez (Eds.), *Bilingual education: Issues and strategies* (pp. 141-156). Newbury Park, CA: Sage.

Comprehensive Adult Student Assessment System. (1982). *Life skills survey achievement tests*. San Diego: Author.

Crandall, J. (Ed.). (1987). *ESL through content area instruction: Mathematics, science, and social studies*. Englewood Cliffs, NJ: Prentice Hall and Center for Applied Linguistics.

ESL Teacher Institute. (1990). *Components of CBE/ESL*. Los Alamitos, CA: Association of California School Administrators.

Freeman, D., & Freeman, Y. (1988). *Sheltered English instruction*. Washington, DC: ERIC Clearinghouse on Languages and Linguistics. (ERIC Document Reproduction Service No. ED 301 070)

Hutchinson, T., & Waters, A. (1987). *English for specific purposes: A learning-centered approach*. London: Cambridge University Press.

Kirsch, I.S., & Jungeblut, A. (1986). *Literacy: Profiles of America's young adults*. Princeton, NJ: Educational Testing Service, National Assessment of Educational Progress.

Language and Orientation Resource Center. (1981). *Teaching ESL to nonliterate adults*. Washington, DC: Center for Applied Linguistics.

Language and Orientation Resource Center. (1982). *Teaching ESL to competencies: A departure from a traditional curriculum for adult learners with specific needs*. Washington, DC: Center for Applied Linguistics.

Office of Refugee Resettlement. (1986). *Competency-based mainstream English language training technical assistance resource package (MELT-TAP)*. Washington, DC: U.S. Department of Health and Human Services.

Savage, K.L. (1984, January). *Teaching strategies for developing literacy skills in non-native speakers of English*. Paper presented at the National Adult Literacy Conference, Washington, DC. (ERIC Document Reproduction Service No. ED 240 296)

Savage, K.L. (1989). *Building life skills 3*. White Plains, NY: Longman.

Savage, K.L. (Ed.). (1992a). *Teacher training through video ESL techniques: Life skills reading*. White Plains, NY: Longman.

Savage, K.L. (Ed.). (1992b). *Teacher training through video ESL techniques: Narrative reading*. White Plains, NY: Longman.

Savage, K.L., with Howe, M., & Yeung, E.L. (1982). *English that works. Book 1*. Glenview, IL: Scott, Foresman.

Savage, K.L., & Mrowicki, L. (1990). ESL literacy: The stages of reading for ESL students. *TESL Talk, 20*(1), 146-164.

Schaffer, D.L., & Van Duzer, C.H. (1984). *Competency-based teacher education workshops in CBE/ESL*. Arlington, VA: Arlington Education and Employment Program.

Short, D.J. (1991). *How to integrate language and content instruction: A training manual* (2nd ed.). Washington, DC: Center for Applied Linguistics.

Tollefson, J.W. (1989). *Alien words: The reeducation of America's Indochinese refugees*. New York: Praeger.

United States Office of Education. (1978). *Report of the USOE invitational workshop on adult competency education*. Washington, DC: U.S. Government Printing Office.

Widdowson, H.G. (1983). *Learning purpose and learning use*. London: Oxford University Press.

CHAPTER 2

Whole Language in Adult Literacy Education

Pat Rigg, American Language and Literacy
Francis E. Kazemek, Eastern Washington University

What does whole language mean to the people who first began applying the term to education? It is not a method, nor is it a collection of strategies, techniques, or materials. Whole language is a view of language and of teaching and learning, a philosophy of education (Edelsky, Altwerger, & Flores, 1991). The term comes not from linguists but from educators, people such as Kenneth and Yetta Goodman, Jerome Harste, and Dorothy Watson, who used it in reference to how children become readers and writers. (See Goodman, 1989; Watson, 1989, for a history of the whole language movement.) They made a number of assertions. The first is that language is whole (hence the name) and that any attempt to fragment it into parts, whether these be grammatical patterns, vocabulary lists, or phonics "families," destroys it. Language must be kept whole or it isn't language anymore.

The second assertion is that, in a literate society, using written language is as natural as using conversation, and the uses of written language develop as naturally as do the uses of oral language (Goodman & Goodman, 1981). We become literate by building on and connecting to our developed oral language. The four language modes, speaking, writing, listening, and reading, are mutually supportive and must not be artificially separated. They should be integrated during instruction, because oral language supports reading and writing; reading exposes us to a wide variety of styles, formats, and conventions; and writing helps us understand how authors put texts together, which in turn helps us read with greater facility.

Third, all language reflects cognitive, emotional, social, and personal differences. Who and what we are is determined in great part by our language. Because we are all unique with an infinite number of different life experiences, our oral and written language often reflect those differences. This is termed "style" or "voice" in composition; it is the idiosyncratic use of language that marks what we say or write as our own.

Fourth, all language, oral and written, is social as well as personal. Although each of us is an individual, all of us are social beings too. We develop our language in a myriad number of social contexts. We learn to speak and listen as we interact with other people, and, likewise, we learn to write and read as we connect with other writers and readers (Gaber-Katz & Watson, 1991).

These four tenets lead to related principles of teaching and learning. Primary among these is the principle that instruction must build on and connect to an individual's life and language experiences. Unless students can make the bridge between their own language and experiences and those in the texts they are attempting to read and write, they will encounter difficulty and frustration.

Participatory is the term used by some adult educators who want their classrooms to be a community of learners and who believe that student choice, student input to curriculum, and student self-evaluation are vital. Participatory teachers often cite the teachings of Paulo Freire, from whom they have learned that literacy is much more than decoding someone else's message. Literacy can be empowering and "liberating" because it gives adult students ways to understand and to alter their worlds (Freire, 1970; Freire & Macedo, 1987; see also Spener, this volume). Excellent examples of participatory materials include Canada's Participatory Research Group's *The Women's Kit,* a set of materials for promoting discussion, literacy, and social change; *Voices Rising,* an international newsletter of women in adult programs published in Toronto; student-dictated books from the East End Literacy program in Toronto; and *Connections,* an annual publication of student work from Boston's Adult Literacy Resource Institute. [See also Peyton, this volume, for information about where other learner-generated materials can be ordered. Eds.]

Whole language advocates assert that oral and written language experiences must be purposeful, functional, and real. Reading and writing activities in the adult literacy classroom must be for purposes of authentic communication, such as to entertain, to convince, to explore, or to excuse oneself. Practice exercises from workbooks that are not authentic uses of language must be avoided (Edelsky, 1987). Thus, complete and whole texts, such as whole stories and complete newspaper articles, must be used for reading. For writing, letters that are mailed, stories that are shared with real audiences, and directions to real locations are excellent sources of authentic communication.

Writing and reading, like speaking and listening, proceed from whole to part. Thus, comprehension of written text leads to an awareness and knowledge of sound-symbol correspondences (phonics). We can make meaningful generalizations about these correspondences only after we understand what we've read and not the other way around. Likewise, the actual writing of meaningful text leads to a knowledge of grammar, spelling generalizations, and so on.

There is no set hierarchy of skills or experiences that all adults must master in sequence. Reading and writing are complex and, in many respects, simultaneous processes: They cannot be broken down into tiny, isolated skills that are then taught in a hierarchical and linear manner. Readers and writers, even those who are very proficient, often cannot articulate or demonstrate specific skills or competencies. Our language competence is almost never captured by our language performance: We always know more than we are able to display at any given time. Similarly, we can be quite competent readers and writers and still be unable to talk about reading and writing using technical terms such as "gerund" or "digraph" or "paragraph transition."

Assessment and evaluation of whole language must itself be holistic (Harp, 1991). We cannot assess growth by using some standardized or criterion-referenced test that measures isolated, partial, or purposeless language skills. To do so would be like evaluating the quality of an apple by using standards typically applied not even to oranges, but to plastic spoons.

Whole Language Principles = Whole Language Classrooms

Applying these basic principles results in whole language classes. Such classes consist of communities of learners, with students negotiating the curriculum and with evaluation as much the students' responsibility as the teacher's (Goodman, Goodman, & Hood, 1989). Whole language advocates are not the first to assert this: Malcolm Knowles (1980), more than a decade ago, laid out the principles of adult education, principles that often read like a whole language manifesto. More recently, Nunan's *Learner-Centered Curriculum*

(1988) and Auerbach's *Making Meaning, Making Change* (1992) present in detail how students and teachers together can negotiate the curriculum.

A class is a community of learners. Whole language teachers work to build a sense of community in the classroom, and they view themselves as co-learners with their students. These teachers do not hold the traditional "jug-and-mug" view of teacher/student roles, with the teacher as a jug full of knowledge and the students as empty mugs waiting to be filled (Auerbach, 1991). Whole language teachers encourage collaboration, having students work together in a variety of ways. Students use both oral and written language as they cooperate to accomplish their goals. Teachers work with their students and with their colleagues in similar ways.

Whole language teachers tie the classroom community to the larger community outside the school building. Parents, grandparents, children, and other members of the community spend time in the classroom as experts on some topic—as storytellers, as observers, and as important contributors to the education of the community both in and out of the classroom (Gaber-Katz & Watson, 1991).

How do whole language principles guide the adult literacy curriculum? The activities described below are not a prescribed list to be followed; rather, they are simply illustrative of how whole language principles might be used to develop meaningful teaching and learning scenarios. There are many different strategies and sequences that might be followed in a whole language classroom. The theoretical perspective is primary; the specific activities grow out of that.

Whole Language Activities

Daily Reading and Writing
Adults who are becoming proficient in reading and writing need to engage in meaningful practice on a daily basis. The silent reading and rereading of self-selected materials should begin or end each class session. At the beginning of the class, these silent reading sessions might last only five minutes. The text should be something in which the adult is interested. Materials that might be used include a Language Experience Approach (LEA) text that the adult or the class dictated and the instructor scribed; or a book, poem, magazine, or newspaper. (The instructor supplies or helps students find appropriate texts.) The adult doesn't have to be able to read all the

words. Similarly, a few minutes devoted to sustained writing in a personal journal about a topic, an event, or one's feelings will help adults experience how they can use writing to organize and express their ideas and emotions. Spelling, grammar, and punctuation are not important in such writing.

Prepared Oral Reading as a Social Activity

Oral reading allows adults to experience the rhythms, perhaps rhyme, and "feel" of written language. All oral reading should be a practiced performance after a good deal of silent reading and oral rehearsal. Oral readings rehearsed with a partner or small group provide the individual with support and peer models; this is especially important for the adult who is learning English as a second language. There are many variations of prepared oral readings, such as choral reading, jazz chants, raps, poems with alternating voices, and readers' theatre. Such reading develops camaraderie, confidence, and an "ear" for spoken texts.

Additionally, the teacher should read to the class on a regular basis. The kinds of texts that can be used are many: LEA texts, poems, popular songs, folktales, lists from newspapers, directions, recipes, and so forth. ESL students can develop an ear for written English by listening to good literature read aloud—poems, chapters of a novel, or short stories. Often, listening to written English read aloud precedes the ESL students' oral reading.

Language Experience Texts

Group-composed and dictated texts that are scribed by the instructor can be meaningful reading materials that provide discussion about aspects of reading and writing, and explorations of society and the world. The Brazilian educator Paulo Freire says that learning to read the word is really learning to read the world (Freire & Macedo, 1987). Group LEA activities allow adults to explore issues, ideas, feelings, and experiences among themselves. These activities can foster group solidarity. Once discussed, the students then translate their oral language into written text. The form that the written text takes is diverse: It can be oral history, narrative, poetry, a song, a letter to an editor or policymaker, directions on how to do or make something, among others. The instructor not only serves as a model by reading and rereading the text, but also points out the difference between oral and written language. Moreover, through the LEA process, the instructor gathers informal information about how individuals are developing as readers and writers (Rigg, 1991).

Reading, Rereading, and Retelling Published Texts

LEA is incomplete unless the students make connections between their own texts and other, published texts. Thus, students' own writing, dictated or otherwise, needs to be complemented with a wide and rich assortment of other materials. For example, an LEA text detailing experiences during a refugee family's escape from civil war can be connected with a book (or other selection) about war and escape from a war-torn area. A group poem about faded friendship can be compared with a poem about the loss of friendship. These connections foster a great deal of reading, rereading (orally and silently, individually and with a partner or group), and, importantly, retelling. Research has shown that the more we retell what we have read, the better we understand it (Rigg & Taylor, 1979). Retellings can be as simple as telling someone else what you have read or jotting down what the text means to you in a journal. Retelling contributes to social interaction and also allows the instructor and student to assess how well the student is constructing meaning from a particular text.

Strategy Instruction

Based on the students' reading, writing, speaking, and listening as demonstrated in the activities just described, the instructor can develop appropriate strategy lessons. These lessons deal with specific aspects of the reading and writing processes that adults need to develop further. For example, the instructor might model how conscious use of background knowledge, context, and understanding of sound-symbol correspondence, used together, can help a reader guess the meaning of an unknown word. Or the instructor might demonstrate how reading in "chunks" instead of word-by-word tends to improve comprehension. Additionally, the instructor might explore with the students how a visual sketch, map, or organizer can help students gather and arrange ideas before they begin to write or read. The important things about strategy lessons are that they follow from and build on what adults are actually doing with language and that they are introduced only when needed.

Evaluation

Whole language classrooms typically use student self-evaluation as part of ongoing and informal assessment that allows the instructor and student to document growth and to plan for future instruction. Because students themselves establish their goals, students themselves monitor their progress (Brindley, 1986). Informal assessment strategies are various:

- keeping anecdotal records of what a student does in particular reading and writing situations
- listening to how students read different kinds of texts
- having students listen to themselves read on tape
- conferring with students about their reading and writing, noting difficulties, efficient strategies, personal goals, types of texts they need or want to read and write
- preparing a checklist of specific things that the teacher and the student want to accomplish during a specific time period
- collecting samples of the student's reading (perhaps on tape, using some type of miscue analysis for evaluation) and writing and charting growth over time
- conducting writing conferences and keeping writing portfolios to help students and the teacher keep track of each person's writing.

Model Whole Language Programs

Which programs for adults learning English language and literacy demonstrate whole language views in practice? At the Bilingual Community Literacy Training Project in Boston, Haitian Creole speakers become literate in their own language and then become the teachers for others of their community (Auerbach, 1991); English literacy thus builds on first language literacy. In two programs in New York City, at the International Ladies' Garment Workers' Union and at the Amalgamated Clothing and Textile Workers Union, both Spanish and English are developed, and the importance of functional literacy and community involvement are stressed (Spener, Lawlar, Wong, Balliro, & Jurmo, 1991). Another union program in the Midwest (described by Soifer, Young, & Irwin, 1989) has clear, functional uses for writing and reading in English.

New Writers' Voices (not to be confused with *VOICES: New Writers for New Readers*) is a series of books from Literacy Volunteers of New York City, each telling about an adult student's memories. East End Literacy Press in Toronto also publishes student autobiographies, focusing especially on women's stories. Aguirre International recently completed a study of model adult ESL education programs in the United States and has published *Bringing Literacy to Life: Issues and Options in Adult ESL Literacy,* which describes several whole language programs (Wrigley & Guth, 1992).

Following is a description of one program that models the whole language philosophy in practice (although the term is not much used there). This program produces *VOICES: New Writers for New Readers. VOICES* is a magazine of adult student writing, but it is much more: It is a demonstration that the newly literate have a great deal to say and have the ability to say it, to write it, and to read it. Unlike many adult ESL programs, which require hours of drills on skills before allowing any authentic interaction with written English, this program starts students writing from the first day, making clear that the instructors believe that the new student, whether a native on nonnative speaker of English, has something important to say and has the ability to say it in writing.

The Invergarry Learning Centre is in Surrey, British Columbia. There are approximately 22,000 people in this high-density neighborhood, with about 50% of the households headed by single parents. This working-class suburb of Vancouver has high unemployment. Much of the area is project housing for single families. Many families speak English as a second or additional language. The Centre offers inexpensive, professional child care so that young parents, especially young mothers, are not prevented from attending.

About half of the adults at Invergarry Learning Centre speak English as an additional language, with proficiency ranging from beginning to near-native fluency. Literacy skills range from no apparent knowledge of the alphabet to fluent reading, although not fluent writing in English. The age range of students is 17 to 80 years of age, with the majority of students in their 20s, 30s, and 40s.

Any adult seeking help in reading or writing is welcome at Invergarry Learning Centre. Often the first contact is a phone call from the adult, seeking information. A trained interviewer talks with the newcomer. The prospective student is not required to have failed any grade or test, nor is a battery of tests administered. Discussions with the interviewer indicate the newcomer's background and establish the newcomer's goals and expectations. The newcomer identifies what he or she wants, and the interviewer clarifies expectations and how the program works.

During the first sessions, the student tours the Centre, finding out what is available, from the variety of classes to the variety of reading materials. Students are encouraged to try reading whatever interests them. "Try three or four pages; see if you want to continue," they are advised. Teachers and tutors may recommend a book, story, or poem once they know a student and feel that this material matches the student's interest, but no one tells a student what to read or what not to read. Books are not selected or suggested on the basis of "levels" or readability formulae. The library is supplied primarily through a book distribution warehouse; the Centre spends from $2,000 to $3,000 (Canadian) a year on materials for the library. The library is as eclectic as possible, containing literature by Atwood, Dostoyevsky, García Márquez, and Steinbeck, for example, as well as Gothic romances, Western novels, mysteries, and cookbooks.

New students are handed a blank, lined notebook and asked to write whatever they want. If they feel themselves unable to write yet, they can dictate what they want to communicate using LEA procedures (Rigg, 1991). [See also Taylor, this volume. Ed.] The notebook is the student's text: She or he will fill it with writing, and that writing will serve as reading material. More importantly, this writer's notebook becomes many adults' first experience using written language to discover what they mean, learning about themselves by writing about themselves (Calkins, 1991).

Students choose a seat at one of the round tables at which three to four other students and their tutors or teachers are sitting— writing, reading, and talking. Conversations occur naturally, focusing on literacy and its connection to each student's life. Students are told about the creative writing group that meets in the evenings and are invited and encouraged to join the group. Evening and day students nurture each other.

The students and tutors (some of them volunteers) move from table to table frequently, so that every student works with more than one person. Students select the people they want to work with and they select different people at different times, sometimes asking another student to respond to their writing, sometimes asking a teacher or tutor. Volunteers receive both formal and informal training. As observers at the round tables, they see and hear how the teachers nurture the students' writing and reading, and thus learn partly by example. The sense of community is strong because each person, whether student, teacher, or tutor, is a writer and discusses writing with the others. Often a student's comment helps a teacher or tutor with his or her own writing, just as a teacher's or tutor's question or comment helps a newly literate student. Each person who responds to a piece of writing offers a different perspective, so students' views of their writing are expanded. This contrasts strikingly with some volunteer adult literacy programs in the United States, where one tutor and one student join in a donor-receiver relationship (Kazemek, 1988) and thus build student dependency.

Teachers and tutors focus on the meaning of the students' writing, which is often autobiographical. The Australian A.B. Facey became literate in order to write his autobiography. His *A Fortunate Life* (1981) is not only a grand book to read but also a testimonial to the idea that adults become literate as they find their voices as writers, and they find their voices as they tell their own stories. To help new writers feel comfortable telling their stories, teachers and tutors tell their own stories, giving some of themselves in order to get some of their students' stories. This is the whole language ideal—teachers and students learning with and from each other in an adult context.

The students soon discover for themselves that sometimes their writing is not clear, and they begin to ask how to change what they previously were comfortable with. An ESL speaker from Brazil, for example, after six months of writing in his new language, became concerned with points of English style, and his notebook testifies to his progress. Student self-evaluation is both constant and easy: Because the students focus on telling their stories as clearly as possible, they continuously rework their material.

Students can submit their writing to *VOICES*. The possibility of publication in an internationally recognized magazine gives students authentic reasons for both revising and editing. More importantly, when a new writer sees her work in the magazine, often with her photograph alongside, her view of herself is changed forever. She is an author, a published author, not really different from the people whose books are on the library shelves.

The Invergarry Learning Centre does not use the term whole language to describe its approach, but the whole language perspective clearly pervades the adult programs there. As a former staff member says, "Our way is too simple for many people: We believe that we learn to read by reading and we learn to write by writing, and we have to pursue both aggressively." The result is a community of writers and learners. Students not only articulate their own goals but also select the materials, activities, and even the people with whom they will work. Teachers and students continually evaluate their own work and collaborate to make it better. No wonder the program is considered a model.

References

Auerbach, E. (1991). Moving on: From learner to teacher. *Literacy 2000: Make the next ten years matter* [Conference summary]. New Westminster, British Columbia, Canada: Douglas College.

Auerbach, E. (1992). *Making meaning, making change: Participatory curriculum development for adult ESL literacy*. McHenry, IL and Washington, DC: Delta Systems and Center for Applied Linguistics.

Brindley, G. (1986). *The assessment of second language proficiency: Issues and approaches*. Adelaide, South Africa: National Curriculum Resource Centre.

Calkins, L. (1991). *Living between the lines*. Portsmouth, NH: Heinemann.

Edelsky, C. (1987). *Writing in a bilingual program: Había una vez*. Norwood, NJ: Ablex.

Edelsky, C., Altwerger, B., & Flores, B. (1991). *Whole language: What's the difference?* Portsmouth, NH: Heinemann.

Facey, A.B. (1981). *A fortunate life*. Ringwood, Victoria, Australia: Penguin Books Australia.

Freire, P. (1970). The adult literacy process as cultural action for freedom. *Harvard Educational Review, 40*, 205-221.

Freire, P., & Macedo, D. (1987). *Literacy: Reading the word and the world*. South Hadley, MA: Bergin & Harvey.

Gaber-Katz, E., & Watson, G. (1991). Combining practice and theory in community literacy. *Literacy 2000: Make the next ten years matter.* [Conference summary]. New Westminster, British Columbia, Canada: Douglas College.

Goodman, K.S. (1989). Roots of the whole language movement. *Elementary School Journal, 90*(2), 113-127.

Goodman, K., & Goodman, Y. (1981). *A whole language comprehension centered view of reading development: A position paper.* (Occasional Papers No. 1). Tucson: University of Arizona, College of Education, Program in Language & Literacy.

Goodman, K., Goodman, Y., & Hood, W. (1989). *The whole language evaluation book.* Portsmouth, NH: Heinemann.

Harp, B. (Ed.). (1991). *Evaluation and assessment in whole language programs.* Norwood, MA: Christopher-Gordon.

Harste, J., Woodward, V., & Burke, C. (1984). *Language stories and literacy lessons.* Portsmouth, NH: Heinemann.

Kazemek, F.E. (1988). Necessary changes: Professional involvement in adult literacy programs. *Harvard Educational Review, 58,* 464-487.

Knowles, M.S. (1980). *The modern practice of adult education: From pedagogy to adragogy.* Chicago: Association Press/Follett.

Nunan, D. (1988). *The learner-centered curriculum: A study in second language teaching.* Cambridge: Cambridge University Press.

Rigg, P. (1991). Using the language experience approach with ESL adults. *TESL Talk, 20*(1), 188-200.

Rigg, P., & Taylor, E. (1979). Measures of comprehension: Independence and implications. In *Monograph in reading and language studies no. 3: New perspectives on comprehension* (pp. 77-83). Bloomington: Indiana University, School of Education.

Soifer, R., Young, D.L., & Irwin, M. (1989). The academy: A learner-centered workplace literacy program. In A. Fingeret & P. Jurmo (Eds.), *Participatory literacy education* (pp. 65-72). San Francisco: Jossey-Bass.

Spener, D., Lawlar, M., Wong, R., Balliro, L., & Jurmo, P. (1991, March). *Participatory practices in workplace ESL: The route to empowerment.* Paper presented at the convention of Teachers of English to Speakers of Other Languages, New York.

Watson, D. (1989). Defining and describing whole language. *Elementary School Journal, 90*(2), 129-141.

Wrigley, H.S., & Guth, G.J.A. (1992). *Bringing literacy to life: Issues and options in adult ESL literacy.* San Mateo, CA: Aguirre International.

CHAPTER 3

The Language Experience Approach

Marcia L. Taylor
JobLink 2000

Language develops from a personal need to communicate not only to survive, but also to express feelings and relate experiences. Language occurs only in social and cultural settings. It must make sense to all involved in the communication process. These basic precepts of language are the foundation for the Language Experience Approach (LEA).

LEA is a whole language approach to instruction that promotes reading and writing by transcribing a student's experiences with the transcription then used as reading material for the student. First developed for native English speaking primary school children, LEA has been used successfully in the English as a second language (ESL) classroom with students of all ages. For purposes of this book, the approach will be presented as a technique for adult ESL students.

History of the Language Experience Approach

The Language Experience Approach is not a modern innovation in the classroom. In fact, it was first introduced at the beginning of this century (Huey, 1908). In the 1960s, it evolved as a technique for elementary school children learning to read (Ashton-Warner, 1963; Spache & Spache, 1964; Stauffer, 1965). In part, it was developed in response to phonetic-based reading instruction, which employs sounds as the building blocks of reading.

Phonetic-based programs teach sound-symbol correspondences, building reading skills around the sounds of the language. Students are able to decode words once they put all of the sound pieces together. This bottom-up, linear approach to reading can be problematic (Smith, 1986). "If the brain had to process letter by letter, by the time we got to the end of long words we would have forgotten the beginning" (Bell & Burnaby, 1988, p. 10). As people read they do not perceive every single letter or word. They actively construct the text using all of their resources. In contrast to phonetic-based instruction, the LEA taps a student's oral language skills and experiences in the world as the foundation for reading and writing.

Kenneth Goodman says that a good teacher acknowledges the fact that the student's wealth of life experience is a tremendous resource. A teacher must recognize that each student comes to school with "a unique set of backgrounds, competencies, skills, sensitivities and needs" (Goodman, 1986).

Banking on this resource, LEA approaches literacy with the whole student in mind, as well as the whole language. Students have an opportunity to see an *entire* text being formed, rather than working exclusively on the development of isolated word-attack skills. They are guided through a discussion of an experience and then on to a transcription of that discussion. Students begin to feel that reading and writing can become as easy and as natural as speech.

A Description of the Language Experience Approach

Although the LEA has been used with many diverse student populations, some characteristics and attributes are consistent for all populations (Hall, 1970):

- Materials are pupil composed.
- All communication skills—reading, writing, speaking, and listening—are integrated.
- Vocabulary and grammar are determined by a student's own grasp of language.
- Learning and teaching are personalized.
- Learning and teaching are communicative.
- Learning and teaching are creative.

Many variations of the basic method have been employed, a few of which are presented in detail here as they apply to adult ESL students. Nonetheless, there are basic similarities to all of the variations:

- The student or group of students orally relate(s) a story or an experience.
- The teacher or "recorder" transcribes this.
- The material generated is first read *to* and later *by* the student(s).

LEA with ESL Students

Krashen and Terrell (1983) define appropriate reading texts for ESL students by two criteria: 1) readings must be at the appropriate level of complexity; and 2) readings must be interesting to the reader. Language experience reading materials meet these two criteria.

Regarding complexity, two ideas should be kept in mind. In his general language theory, Krashen proposes the idea of "comprehensible input" expressed as a simple formula of $i + 1$: A language learner can understand a text that is one step beyond his or her current level of language competency. In order for a student's language to progress, it is necessary for that student to be exposed to language that is challenging and yet understandable.

Second, as Krashen points out, students are able to comprehend grammatical forms that are beyond their active or productive repertoire. Therefore, a teacher need not be overly concerned about grammatical control in reading selections.

Language experience stories are generated by students; the degree of complexity is determined by the students, not by an exterior measure of reading competency. Because the stories relate to students' personal experiences, the texts are likely to be interesting to the authors themselves and to other student readers. Transcribing the student's story using a word processor is ideal. The transcription goes quickly, and the finished product looks professional. Students are proud of stories that have been printed in this way, and they often comment that they will share it with their families.

LEA with Adult ESL Students

Many students who enter adult ESL classes have well developed speaking skills but only low-level literacy skills. The LEA is ideal with such students because it capitalizes on their strengths and speaking skills and allows students' reading to evolve from their spoken language.

This approach also addresses a common concern in adult ESL classes: finding texts for beginning adult readers that are appropriate and interesting. Many texts written in simplified English are juvenile, uninteresting, or even demeaning to adult readers. Using the LEA circumvents this problem.

Two Variations of LEA

Personal Experience

The personal experience approach is the original form of the LEA. A student relates a personal experience to a teacher, aide, or volunteer who transcribes the experience. The transcriber reads the experience to the student and the student then reads it. To be more specific:

1. The transcriber sits next to, not across from, the student so that the student can read what is being written or typed.

2. The session begins with a conversation, from which a topic to write about develops. Questions from the transcriber help generate topics for the story. Such questions might address what the student did the night before or over the weekend, something the student misses from home, a special person, or a frightening experience.

The following story was dictated by a beginning ESL student in a workplace literacy program.

José Works on a Farm

I live on a farm. When I was a little boy, my mother put me in school. When it was harvest time, they took me out of school to pick corn and garbanzos and wheat. We had a lot of potatoes and vegetables and onions.

That's when I lost whatever I learned in school. Then two months later I'd go back to school again. Like in February, we'd pick tomatoes and in May, garbanzo beans. So in the year I didn't learn too much.

Although this process may sound simple, there are two factors that are important for its success. To begin with, a relationship of trust between the learner and the teacher must already be established. Writing about a personal experience is very similar to writing in a diary. The intrusion of someone into this personal process can be inhibiting. Ideally, the teacher should be tolerant, warm, and patient.

Second, the teacher must decide how to transcribe the student's language. Should the teacher correct the student's language or write it with the student's errors? Originally, and in the purest form of the LEA, a teacher writes the experience exactly as the student dictates it. The errors made are simple testimony of the student's language development at that time. Student errors are a natural part of the language development process and evidence of the student's oral language level. Documentation from continued use of this approach provides concrete evidence of the oral growth of the student's language (Heald-Talyor, 1989).

In contrast, some educators (Hunter, 1982) believe that writing an error on the board or on a page reinforces it. Proponents of this philosophy correct errors as quickly as possible. Hunter suggests modeling rather than overtly correcting. For example, if a student says, "We go to the store yesterday," the teacher could respond, "We go to the store often. And yesterday, we went to the store." This kind of paraphrasing is one way of correcting or modeling the appropriate form. (The dictated story shown above was corrected by the teacher.)

The issue of error correction can also be addressed in another way, and is discussed in the following section on group experience.

Group Experience

LEA can also be used with group experiences, which evolve naturally or are staged for and with the class. After the group participates in a situation, the students compose a story, retelling the experience. Although this variation may require a good deal of planning, it can be easier to implement because it does not require the one-to-one transcription that a personal experience does. The following steps describe the process from planning to follow-up.

1. *Choose the experience.* Choose a field trip or a classroom activity that can later be discussed and written as a story. Common experiences might be taking a trip to the bank or making popcorn. Involve the students at this stage by asking them to choose the experience. The possibilities may be limited by saying, "Let's make lunch on Tuesday. What do you suggest we make?"

Allowing students to choose the activity ensures that the approach is geared to adults. They may not want to cook or prepare anything in class. Try other topics or ask them for ideas. Voting on the choices involves students in the democratic process and promotes student interest in the experience.

2. *Organize the experience.* Develop a plan of action with the students. The plan should include the activity and the items needed. Students may be asked to bring in special supplies or ingredients. A plan of action should be written on the board. Whether it's a schedule or a list of ingredients, the basic vocabulary for organizing an

experience is the first link between the experience and the written word.

3. *Conduct the experience.* When feasible, narrate the steps that are taking place as everyone participates in the experience. The language used should be clear and concise, with repetition of key words and phrases. The selected words and phrases may be written on the board before beginning the experience.

4. *Discuss the experience.* Follow the activity with a discussion of the steps or sequence of events that took place. Be sure that all students participate in some way. Some students may be capable of giving a running account of the experience, while others may have to be pulled into the discussion by asking them to respond with brief responses to questions such as, "Who helped us at the post office?"

It is inevitable that students with greater speaking ability will contribute more at this point. Nonetheless, it is crucial that all students understand the discussion. Because discussion and follow-up of the experience can be conducted at different ability levels, the LEA is ideal in multilevel classrooms. With students at beginning English language and literacy levels, stories may be very simple, perhaps only a sentence or two. If this represents the English proficiency of the class, it is appropriate. Length is not important.

5. *Compose the language experience story.* Rather than have each student dictate his or her story to the teacher or aide, students compose a group story. Students dictate the steps or sequence of events that took place, and a teacher or aide writes their words where all the students can easily see them: on a board, a flip chart pad, or an overhead transparency. This version of the story will be referred to in the future. The overhead transparency allows for duplicate copies of the story for each student, which they can then read independently. (The teacher makes photocopies of the transparency.)

How closely should the students' language be followed? Because the benefits of writing the students' language verbatim may no longer be valid in a group effort, the instructor may decide not to include incorrect speech. Instead, as a group-written piece is being created, the instructor paraphrases statements or helps students formulate their thoughts. Asking for group participation is also a good strategy.

Using phrases such as, "Maybe we can say it like this," or "How else could we say it?" softens the corrections.

6. *Read the story.* Once the story is completed, students read it through. Begin this process by reading the story aloud and underlining key words and phrases. Review those words with students and then have them read the story with you.

7. *Follow-up activities.* Have students read the story the next day and even the next week to check for retention. In addition, the following activities can be integrated into the experience:

• Select words from the story to be used for a vocabulary or a spelling list.

• Delete every fifth word to create a cloze exercise. This is easy to do if you have used an overhead transparency. Make a photocopy, and starting with the second sentence, white out every fifth word, making a list of the words deleted. First, have students fill in the blanks from the list of words provided. Next, have them complete the sentences without consulting the list.

• Rewrite the story, changing the order of the sentences. Have students put the sentences in the correct order.

• Write the story, word by word, on cards. Have students work in groups to recreate it.

• Scramble some of the key words and have students unscramble them.

• Have students group words in the story with the same beginning sounds.

• Have students match words with pictures.

Sample Experiences

Making Submarine Sandwiches

1. *Choose the experience.* If the class has chosen to have lunch, dinner, or a hefty snack, making submarine sandwiches can be a lot of fun. A few sandwiches will feed a classroom. Students may choose to make sandwiches, but they may not understand what a submarine sandwich is. A drawing or a simple description will clarify this.

2. *Organize the experience.* A general description of the object is necessary. "A submarine sandwich is a very big sandwich. Some are made of two or more kinds of meat, different kinds of cheese, let-

tuce, and other toppings. Let's choose what to put on our sandwiches."

Make a complete list of ingredients and implements necessary to complete the experience. If there is access to an overhead projector or a flip chart, write the list on either of these, making it possible to refer back to it later.

Students should get a copy of the list. Either duplicate the overhead transparency or copy the list from the flip chart or board and then duplicate it, or have students copy it by hand.

After the list is complete, ask students to volunteer to bring in the ingredients. The instructor can bring the ingredients or sundries that haven't been claimed. Then read the list with the class. If the class level is quite basic, draw a picture next to each item to aid comprehension.

Make sure the students understand when the sandwiches will be made. Everyone's participation is crucial.

3. *Conduct the experience*. Bring out the list again and check off the ingredients that have been brought to class. Show each item, ask a student to name it, and point to the word on the list.

The instructor may lead all of the steps of the activity or have a student assist. As the sandwich is being prepared, narrate the actions and write the corresponding verbs on the board, flip chart, or transparency. A student can then write selected words. For example, in the first step, *Take the bread and cut it with a good knife*, a student might help by writing, "1. cut." In the second step, *then spread butter on one side and mayonnaise on the other side*, the assistant would write, "2. spread." It is important to list each step involved in preparation of the meal.

Once the sandwiches are prepared, enjoy! Paper plates, napkins, and an accompaniment, such as carrot sticks, hot peppers, or potato chips, and a beverage round out the meal. All of these should be included in the planning stage.

4. *Discuss the experience*. Ask students questions that arise naturally from the experience. In this case, questions might be, "Do you like submarine sandwiches?" or "Aren't Pepe and Susana good cooks?" Then proceed with questions pertaining to the process, such as, "How did we begin this experience?" Elicit a response that includes the initial preparation. Have any prior written material (the ingredient list or the verb list) in view for vocabulary reference.

5. *Compose the language experience story.* Using an overhead projector, a flip chart, or the chalkboard, ask students for a step-by-step account of making the submarine sandwiches. Again, have the previous lists available for reference.

As students provide the information, record their comments. If students are beginners, number each step. If students are more advanced, form paragraphs from their comments.

6. *Read the story.* Once the story is complete, read it aloud once or twice to students, pointing to the line as it is read. Then have students read the story aloud. Finally, have them read it silently.

7. *Follow-up activities.* Have students read the story aloud the following class period. Prepare activities to take full advantage of the language experience just staged. If the current topic is food, you may want to focus on vocabulary related to food preparation, with flash cards of the food words used in the story. Then pass out the cards to students and have them line up in the preparation sequence; the bread first, then the mayonnaise, the margarine, and so forth. (See also the list of follow-up activities outlined on page 53.)

A Trip to the Post Office

1. *Choose a topic.* Another kind of shared or group experience is the kind that takes place in the community. If the current classroom topic is government, a trip to City Hall may be interesting. If students are learning about communicating by mail, a trip to the post office can be both fun and informative.

2. *Organize the experience.* Before planning with students, be sure to clear any visits with the appropriate sources. In this case, call the director of the local post office and explain when and why the class would like to visit. The post office may provide a tour for students to see the work that goes on behind the scenes. Planning this experience with students entails choosing a day most students will be able to attend. The mode of transportation also must be decided. If going by car, this is the time to plan a car pool.

Tell students to prepare a few questions to ask at the post office. They might ask about how to send money overseas or the difference between various classes of mail. Their questions will depend on their language level and their knowledge of postal services.

3. *Conduct the experience.* Field trips with adults are much less stressful than those with children. Nonetheless, it is important that everyone stay with the group. Assigning people to small subgroups

is sometimes recommended. At the post office, encourage students to ask questions. The instructor can initiate the questions, with students following his or her lead. Be sure to show students where to find postal forms for special services. Ask for class sets of these forms for practice in class.

4. *Discuss the experience.* In the classroom, lead a discussion about the experience. Although the instructor may get students started, students will soon take over. If students find that the walk was the most interesting segment of the post office trip, that's what their story will eventually relate.

5. *Compose the language experience story.* Discussion of this field trip will help get everyone started writing. Students may comment on what was most interesting to them or relate the experience from start to finish. Try to give students free reign in their comments, but always provide structure and vocabulary when asked.

6. *Read the story.* Read the story two or three times. Make sure students follow along. Also have students read aloud. Circle key words, those that are your particular focus, or those that pose difficulties to students.

7. *Follow-up activities.* As always, reading is the first and most important follow-up exercise. In addition to the activities suggested earlier in this chapter, the following might be tried. If forms were collected from the post office, pass them out, discuss their function, and have students fill them out. If a tour guide assisted on the trip into the community, have students write that person a thank you letter. The group writing technique may be used, or students may write individual thank you notes and address their own envelopes.

These are just two samples of possible language experience activities. With the students' help, many more activities can be created. The key is to focus on students' interests, needs, and language levels to make these experiences worthwhile and meaningful.

Other Possible Activities

In the classroom	*In the community*
Making French toast	Planning a trip
Making a salad	(to the bank, city hall,
Making cards	the supermarket)
(thank you notes,	Interpreting signs in and around school
get well cards,	Mapping the neighborhood
holiday cards)	
Filling out a tax form	
Making a LEA folder	

These activities are appropriate for beginning students. For more advanced students, discussions of topics such as those listed below can become group writings.

- Work
- Adult education
- Adjustment to life in the United States

The following activity, *To Change Oil,* was written collaboratively by a group of advanced ESL students in a workplace literacy program, the culmination of a series of such activities. The students knew how to change oil, so they didn't do it in class, but they wrote about the process together.

To Change Oil

To properly change the oil to your automobile, follow these steps.

First of all, you must make sure that you have the proper grade of oil and quantity needed (check your car manual). Also make sure that you have the right filter. Then make sure that you have the proper tools to do the job, such as a filter wrench and sockets for the oil pan plug.

Next consult the automobile manual for the oil filter location. Check and see if the oil filter can be changed from the top. If not, drive the automobile over an 8" ramp for easy access to the oil pan plug and filter. Now you need a container for the dirty oil and filter.

Change the oil by removing the oil pan plug and letting the oil drain. At the same time, remove the oil filter. After all the oil has drained, install the new filter and oil pan plug. Follow the manufacturer's installation procedures. The filter must be hand-tightened only.

Finally, add the new oil and check the oil level before starting the engine. Then start the engine and check for leaks. Turn off the engine and once more check the oil level. Add oil if needed.

Conclusion

Although it is primarily thought of as a tool for literacy development, the LEA helps develop all skills—listening, speaking, reading, and writing—in an integrated manner.

The language experience approach begins with students' own experiences or a shared experience as the basis for discussion and writing. Students talk about the experiences and then see their words transformed into a written text. Connecting these experiences to the written word may be something students have never done before. By giving them this opportunity, the LEA provides a valuable tool in total language development.

References

Ashton-Warner, S. (1963). *Teacher*. New York: Simon & Schuster.

Bell, J., & Burnaby, B. (1988). *A handbook for ESL literacy*. Toronto, Ontario: Ontario Institute for Studies in Education Press.

Goodman, K. (1986). *What's whole in whole language?* Portsmouth, NH: Heinemann.

Hall, M.A. (1970). *Teaching reading as a language experience*. Columbus, OH: Charles Merrill.

Heald-Taylor, G. (1989). *Whole language strategies for ESL students*. San Diego: Dormac.

Huey, E.B. (1908). *The psychology and pedagogy of reading*. New York: Macmillan.

Hunter, M. (1982). *Mastery teaching*. El Segundo, CA: TIP Publications.

Krashen, S.D., & Terrell, T.D. (1983). *The natural approach*. Hayward, CA: Alemany.

Smith, F. (1986). *Understanding reading* (3rd ed.). Hillsdale, NJ: Lawrence Erlbaum.

Spache, G., & Spache, E. (1964). *Reading in the elementary school*. New York: Allyn & Bacon.

Stauffer, R.G. (1965). A language experience approach. In J.A. Kerfoot (Ed.), *First grade reading programs: Perspectives in reading no. 5* (pp. 86-118). Newark, DE: International Reading Association.

CHAPTER 4

Listening to Students' Voices: Publishing Students' Writing for Other Students to Read

Joy Kreeft Peyton
Center for Applied Linguistics

All of us find we have interesting stories to tell about aspects of our lives, if we are in a context where we are supported and encouraged to tell those stories. The life experiences of many adults learning English as a second language (ESL) in this country can be particularly compelling—the traumas of war and flight from their country; the heartaches of missing country, family, and friends; the adjustments to life in new surroundings, whether a crowded refugee camp or cramped public housing; the struggles to understand and use a new language and to enter the social and professional mainstream of an unfamiliar culture. Stories about these experiences can be

> fascinating, enlightening, touching, and inspiring beyond our capacity to imagine. There is a sweet sadness, an intense excitement, and a window to the world to be revealed if refugees and immigrants to the U.S. can be encouraged to tell their stories and to share them with [others]. (Rawlston, 1988, p. 1)

At the same time, these stories can be a powerful learning tool for adults enrolled in ESL, literacy, and general education programs. Educators who encourage and help their students express their life events orally or in writing and publish those accounts as materials for other students to read find that this activity benefits both writers and readers. This chapter presents the rationale for using the writings of adult ESL students as material for teaching literacy to other ESL adults, outlines the steps involved in implementing a writing and publishing program, and gives sources of published materials written by adult literacy learners and descriptions of student publishing programs.

Benefits to Writers and Readers
of Publishing Student Work

Students who publish their writings within or beyond the classroom experience many benefits. They discover that the realities of their own lives are worth thinking about, getting down on paper, and sharing with others. When they see their thoughts and concerns and those of others like them in print, they find that they can have a powerful voice and play a vital role in their new culture. Sharon Howell Cox, a writer and writing teacher at the Jefferson Park Writing Center in Cambridge, Massachusetts, has stated, "Everybody deserves a voice. . . . [Nobody] in the culture should have more of a voice than the next person" (quoted in Martin, 1989, p. 7). As student writers find that others are interested in and can benefit from their thoughts and experiences, they are motivated to express themselves in more interesting, worthwhile, and readable ways. As they work with all aspects of language use, from effective genres and discourse structures to correct grammar and punctuation, they are "drawn into a meaningful relationship with English" (Rawlston, 1988). Finally, writing for publication and reading the writing of their peers provides students with many opportunities to reflect on what constitutes good writing.

One teacher's account of the publication of a class magazine dramatically illustrates the positive impact that publishing can have on adult ESL writers.

Promising my students that their writing would be published in a class magazine had been a time-honored technique of mine to generate excitement in my writing classes. However, when I made the same promise to my newly formed ESL writing classes, my students were less than enthusiastic; they were politely indifferent. It was not until days later I discovered the reasons: The students did not believe me, and they did not believe they had anything to say in English because they could not write perfectly. . . . But as we struggled through the first writing assignments, I rejoiced as I saw the tentative beginnings of their voices, powerful voices struggling for the words to speak their hearts. . . .

Trust deepened in my students and so did the resonance in their voices. Their voices, now just a quiet whisper, spoke of survival in spite of war, of grief for lost family and country, of happiness and frustration in their new lives. Those whispers were written to me only; I hoped soon those whispers could touch more hearts than my own. . . .

At the beginning of second semester, my students' voices were singing, laughing, and crying; I knew it was time to publish. I reminded them that if writing really communicated, if it really spoke to people's hearts, then our writing was ready to speak in our magazine. . . .

[When 500 copies of the magazine were published] I pulled out a copy and flashed it; the students sat silently for a few seconds and then erupted into a chorus of cheers. After scrapping the lesson plan for the day, we had a publishing party. The students read their stories to each other; they laughed together; they cried together; they celebrated together. Then I just watched and marveled as they asked their friends to autograph the pieces each had written.

We wrote a cover letter and presented our magazine as a gift to relatives, teachers, administrators, district board members, and other ESL classes in other districts. For many days after, students shared the compliments they received from teachers and students; they laughed that so many asked if the war stories were true, yet they were grateful for the opportunity to share their experiences with their new friends.

My students finally understood that even though they were still learning the English language, their developing voices were powerful and strong. Finally, they saw the evidence for the truth of the proverb our classes had adopted:

> Life and love are like young rice;
> Transplanted, they still grow.

My students, with their transplanted lives, hearts, and voices, had grown, and now they were helping others to grow.

This year began differently. This year my students asked, "How soon do we begin our magazine? (Nishizaki, 1984, pp. 15 & 16)

There are also distinct benefits for the readers of student-produced materials. Learners often find these stories more interesting and easier to read than other published materials because they see their own struggles reflected, and the language used is often more accessible. Commercially produced texts available for use in adult literacy programs may contain material far removed from the realities that adult learners face, and the simple topics and language structures may hold little interest or cognitive challenge for them (Auerbach & Burgess, 1985). Student-produced materials can form a body of contemporary knowledge, presenting a more authentic view of learners' struggles, triumphs, and feelings of dislocation, and can affirm their capacity to function as adults making intelligent decisions.

Many students, especially beginning readers, come to class with doubts as to whether, as adults, they truly can become successful learners. Seeing the successes of others like them, who have struggled and succeeded, gives them models and concrete evidence that it can be done and inspires them to write their own stories.

Teachers and policy makers can also benefit from these writings. Research on retention in adult literacy programs has shown that many students stop attending classes because they feel their needs are not being met (Brod, 1990; Hunter & Harman, 1979). When students write about the literacy issues they face, their reasons for attending school, and their perceptions of a program's effectiveness (as a group of students did in the book *Where Do We Go From Here?*, included in the list of available materials at the end of this chapter), educators and policy makers have information that can help them plan programs that are more responsive to students' needs and interests and to their lives outside the classroom.

Finally, literacy program developers can benefit from having these materials, because they "provide a source of inexpensive and creative reading material where materials are direly needed" (Gaber-Katz & Horsman, 1988, p. 119).

Steps to Implementing a Writing and Publishing Program

The past decade has seen a revolution in views about teaching writing, the major change being a shift in focus from the written product to the writing process. The work of teacher/researchers such Lucy Calkins (1983, 1986), Donald Graves (1983), Nancie Atwell (1987) with elementary students, and Donald Murray (1982) with adults, has had a profound effect on writing approaches with all students, including adults learning English literacy. In addition, adult ESL literacy educators have written in detail about their writing and publishing programs (see citations for program descriptions at the end of this chapter). The brief guidelines given here are informed by those sources, which should be consulted by anyone wishing to set up such a program.

Encouraging Students to Write

The writing process involves time and many opportunities to think through ideas and discuss them with others, to draft text, discuss, revise, draft more, and discuss and revise more until a piece emerges with which the writer and readers are satisfied and that can be edited, published, and distributed.

Students of all ages and English proficiency levels, even at very beginning stages of literacy learning, can become actively involved in writing and publishing their work, but they may need a tremendous amount of support and encouragement to do so (as the account by Nishizaki, above, shows clearly). Early in the course, it is important to assure students that they have interesting experiences and valuable ideas that are worth writing about and that, working together, they will be able to express themselves in writing. They will also benefit from discussions on the nature of the writing process—how difficult writing can be at times, even for native speakers of a language, and how many drafts writers might write and rewrite before they have a polished piece. Students need to be encouraged not to despair when their words don't flow as automatically as they might like them to.

Getting Started: Prewriting

Before students ever begin to write, a tremendous amount of talk about what might be written is essential, especially with students who are struggling with the language and believe they have nothing to say. As Sharon Howell Cox describes,

> Writing doesn't [just] happen. . . . It happens, like, you talk about it, you start to think about it. You may not think of it connected to a piece. And then you get a little more information or you do a little more talking within the group. And someone says this and you say that and by the time it's all over, you have an idea of something, and it starts to bother you and nag you and then it comes out in some form. It takes some shape. People play off each other, and they're stimulated or they're made mad or. . . . It's all stimulus. (quoted in Martin, 1989, p. 7)

In one-on-one sessions with the teacher or another student or in a group setting, students might explore different topics, ideas, and directions, considering issues such as the following:

What experiences, activities, ideas, topics they are interested in.

What topics they feel they know a lot about.

What they would like to learn.

What they would like to explore.

(From Publishing an Anthology of Adult Student Writing, 1985, p. 18).

If students are writing autobiographical narratives, they might talk about leaving their country, experiences in the new country, problems they have had, or hurdles they have overcome. They might also consider other genres such as essay writing, document and technical writing, or poetry and fiction.

Artifacts such as drawings, photographs, and favorite objects from home, the community, or the native country might be brought in to provide stimulus for the writing (Wallerstein, 1983). Family and community histories, traditional music, and myths and beliefs that have been transmitted orally are also a rich source of ideas, and when captured in print, they preserve and validate the knowledge and practices of a group, language, or culture (Gillespie, 1989).

Students might interview each other, read stories aloud, and read the writing of other students—possibly students from preceding years in the program—to stimulate ideas.

Drafting

Much of the drafting process is also exploratory. Students need to know at this point that they are not producing finished, polished text but are still exploring ideas, now in print. They might free write, putting down anything that comes to mind about the topic they have chosen; generate lists; write a letter to a friend or a journal entry to the teacher about their topic—whatever helps them to get their ideas in print. Eventually an idea will begin to take shape, and the student can begin to move toward producing a draft of a complete piece.

Students with beginning literacy proficiencies may need to dictate their thoughts to a teacher or aide, who writes them down and reads them back to the author. Russell (1985) describes his success drafting passages with beginning writers thus:

I often sat down with the people who were least able to write, for up to an entire class period. "Tell me, just tell me right now," I would say, "why you came to this country." A story gradually unfolded, the person relaxed, and we forgot about the pen and paper in front of us. After the story was finished, I'd say, "How did that story start?" We would begin with the first word of the first sentence. . . . The better writers in the class came to take my place in this process of helping those most afraid of trying. (p. 41)

Sharing and Responding to Writing

Talking with readers and other writers, who respond with questions and suggestions, is important throughout the drafting process, as it is in all stages of writing. Students may share their work with the teacher or peers in the early stages of producing a draft—reviewing an idea, reading sections of text, or hearing parts of another student's drafted sections. Once a completed first draft is ready, they might gather in pairs or small groups for more formal sharing or to read their entire piece aloud and consider questions from listeners.

What's your purpose in this paper?

What are you trying to do in the paper?

What did you learn from writing it?

What do you hope others will learn?

What parts of the paper do you like the best?

What parts did you have trouble with?

(From *Publishing an Anthology of Adult Student Writing*, 1985, p. 19).

Revising

Revising involves further shaping and may be done at several points in the production of a piece. Students who write frequently will probably not choose to revise the drafts of all of their papers but will choose those they or their audiences are particularly interested in and that they plan to publish. Although computers are not essential in a student writing program, they certainly make revising (as well as drafting and editing) much easier. When students are revising, the teacher might want to teach mini-lessons on various aspects of the process—finding a lead or an ending, moving and inserting text, shaping a piece for a particular audience. (See Atwell, 1987, for extensive discussion of various types of mini-lessons.) If students are using computers to revise, it is particularly important that they understand the various functions available to them and how to use them.

Editing

Editing is the final stage of writing, during which the focus is on grammar, punctuation, and sentence structure. A student's entire writing portfolio does not need to be edited, only those pieces that will be published. Students might work in pairs to edit, a student who is more proficient with English working with a less proficient student, or a student who likes to edit and feels competent at it working with one who doesn't (some students have much more interest in and skill with editing than others). This is another time when mini-lessons on particular points of grammar, style, or punctuation might be helpful.

Publication and Distribution

Students may write for many different audiences: class members, their children or other family members, friends, or other people they feel may have experiences similar to their own. Many literacy programs compile student writings into booklets, newsletters, or magazines for classroom distribution, but some programs go a step beyond to publish for a wider audience.

Publishing for an audience beyond the classroom takes considerable planning and organization. Most student publishing programs have an editorial board consisting in part or entirely of students. The board establishes publication schedules and criteria for publishable work. It reads and selects contributions, works with authors in revising and editing their pieces, and puts the publication together. Appropriateness of various types of texts and freedom of expression and censorship are important issues that editorial boards often face.

If graphics and desktop publishing programs are available, students can take a much more active role in getting their work published. They can design their own text layout, create book covers, and in some cases, produce their own books for distribution.

Programs need to develop a system for advertising and distribution and may need to seek additional funds for publication. Martin (1989) provides information about avenues for distribution, such as displaying in local bookstores, listing publications in *Books in Print*, getting works reviewed in community publications, and sending announcement flyers to local libraries. She also lists some sources of funding, such as libraries, local businesses, or the National Endowment for the Humanities.

The following are some of the types of student-written publications—magazines, newspapers, newsletters, and books—that various programs have produced. (See also Rigg, this volume, for others.)

- In Boston, an adult ESL class produced a magazine of student writings and distributed them to native Bostonians so they could better understand the experiences of contemporary immigrants (Russell, 1985).

- The Publishing for Literacy Project, also in Boston, publishes a literary magazine of adult student writings, *Need I Say More*, that is generally available.

- The International Ladies' Garment Workers' Union (ILGWU) in New York City publishes student magazines featuring different themes—life, work, education, and literature. The magazines of one year's students become part of the reading text for students the following year.

- *News and Reviews* is a student newspaper of articles, book reviews, and interviews published by Literacy Volunteers of New York City. *Students Speaking Out* is a newsletter published by Laubach Literacy Action.

- *Tales from Boston Neighborhoods*, a project of the Boston Public Library, publishes a series of books in which adult ESL literacy learners describe community life in Boston. Their goal is to present their own perspectives, to counteract media portrayals of their communities as crime- and drug-ridden ghettos. The books are available in Boston's branch libraries as well as in local bookstores.

- In Pennsylvania, a writing contest for adult basic education and basic literacy students (both native and nonnative English speaking) resulted in the publication of an anthology of selected fiction, nonfiction, and poetry, distributed to literacy project directors across the United States (*Publishing an Anthology of Adult Student Writing*, 1985).

These represent only a few of many current programs and products. Descriptions of several programs, and information on how to obtain various published student materials, are given at the end of this chapter.

Some Words of Caution

ESL educators who have developed successful writing and publishing programs have discovered a number of issues that need to be confronted by anyone wishing to implement such a program.

- Teachers wishing to use a writing process approach with their students need to be trained in these approaches, and they themselves need to write and publish so they understand the challenges their students face.

- A considerable amount of time needs to be devoted to reading and writing to allow students to explore topics, discuss ideas, draft text, and work with each other. Writing for meaning needs to be balanced with a focus on writing conventions such as spelling and grammar.

- Adults who have been socialized to believe that schooling means completing a preplanned curriculum and working with textbooks may need help to overcome feelings that they "aren't learning anything" in an open-ended program.

- If it is necessary to prove to program supervisors and outside funders that "real work" is being accomplished and that students are improving, teachers may want to use writing portfolios and student-centered assessments as records of learning (Marilyn Gillespie, personal communication, December 1989).

Conclusion

Encouraging and helping beginning readers and writers to write for other beginning readers and writers is an exciting new approach with promising potential. Students who see their writings in print, valued by others, experience increased motivation and self-esteem and thus an increased desire to develop their abilities. Not only are authors enriched by getting their thoughts on paper, but those who read their works are enriched by having access to the writers' experiences and are stimulated to share their own. Finally, the published works of student writers provide a rich and compelling body of literature from which ESL adult literacy programs can draw.

Available Student-Published Materials

The following is a sample of the available materials written by or collected as oral histories from adult literacy learners, many of whom were learning English as a second language. Some of these items come from a list compiled by the Family Literacy Project at the University of Massachusetts, Boston (see also Auerbach, 1989, for annotations of these and other materials for adults becoming literate in ESL). In addition to the contacts given, some of these materials are available from the ERIC Document Reproduction Service (EDRS), 7420 Fullerton Road, Suite 110, Springfield, VA 22153-2852, (800) 443-ERIC. In those cases, the ED number for identifying the document is provided.

The Boston Public Library has stories from the *Tales from Boston Neighborhoods* project and *It's Never Easy*, a collection of writings by adult learners. Contact the library's business office or Ellen Graf, Special Projects Librarian, P.O. Box 286, Boston, MA 02117; or Dudley Branch Library, 65 Warren Street, Roxbury, MA 02119.

East End Literacy Press has published a series of books, written by adult literacy learners, available from Pippin Publishing, 150 Telson Road, Markham, Ontario, Canada L3R 1E5.

Family Literacy Project, University of Massachusetts, Boston. *Looking Forward, Looking Back: Writings from Many Worlds.* (1989). Contact Barbara Graceffa, Bilingual/ESL Graduate Studies, University of Massachusetts, Boston, MA 02125-3393.

Gatehouse Press. *Where Do We Go from Here?* (1988). Available from Avanti Books, 1 Wellington Road, Stevenage, Herts, SG2 9HR, England.

Hope Publishing House. *The Story of Ana, La historia de Ana.* Ely Patricia Martínez Vasquez and others. (1986). Available from Hope Publishing House, P.O. Box 60008, Pasadena, CA 91106.

Intercultural Productions. *String Bracelet: Reflections of and by the Young People of Southeast Asia.* (1988). Available from Intercultural Productions, P.O. Box 57343, Washington, DC 20036.

International Ladies' Garment Workers' Union (ILGWU) has a student magazine with sections on life, work, education, and literature. Available from ILGWU, Worker-Family Education Program, 1710 Broadway, New York, NY 10019. (ERIC Document Reproduction Service Nos. ED 313 919 to ED 313 923)

International Task Force on Literacy. *Book Voyage: Personal Accounts of Newly Literate People from Around the World.* (1991). Order from the International Task Force on Literacy, 720 Bathurst Street, Suite 500, Toronto, Ontario, Canada M5S 2R4.

Invergarry Learning Center. *Voices: New Writers for New Readers,* a student-produced magazine. Available from Invergarry Learning Centre, 9260 140th Street, Surrey, British Columbia V3V 5Z4.

Jefferson Park Writing Center. *Hear my Soul's Voice: A Literary Magazine of Adult Student Writings.* Published once a year. Available from Jefferson Park Writing Center, 6 Jefferson Park, Apartment 52, Cambridge, MA 02140.

Laubach Literacy Action. *Students Speaking Out,* a student newsletter. Available from Laubach Literacy Action, 1320 Jamesville Avenue, Syracuse, NY 13210.

Literacy Volunteers of New York City. *Big Apple Journal* and *New Writers' Voices,* a series of books of student writings about home, family, and health. *News and Reviews,* a student newspaper of articles, book reviews, and interviews. Available from Literacy Volunteers of New York City, 121 Avenue of the Americas, New York, NY 10013.

Mosaic. An annual magazine of high school students' autobiographical stories and photographs, published from 1982-1988. Order from Mosaic, 95 G Street, Boston, MA 02127.

New Readers Press. Two collections of oral histories in Spanish, *Cuentos de Lucha y Alegría (Stories of Struggle and Joy)* and *Más Cuentos de Lucha y Alegría (More Stories of Struggle and Joy)* can be ordered from New Readers Press, Publishing Division of Laubach Literacy International, P.O. Box 131, Syracuse, NY 13210.

Opening Doors Books publishes a series of books written by adult basic education students in Vermont. Available from Opening Doors Books, P.O. Box 379, Bristol, VT 05443.

Pennsylvania Adult Basic Education. *Our Words, Our Voices, Our Worlds: Selected Poetry and Prose by Pennsylvania's Adult Basic Education Students.* (ERIC Document Reproduction Service No. ED 260 185)

Publishing for Literacy Project. *Need I Say More: A Literary Magazine of Adult Student Writings.* Available from Kona Khasu, Project Coordinator, Publishing for Literacy, Adult Literacy Resource Institute, c/o Roxbury Community College, 1234 Columbus Avenue,

Boston, MA 02120; or Michael Steinfeld, Public Library of Brookline, 361 Washington Street, Brookline, MA 02146.

Toronto East End Literacy Project has published various student-produced texts, including *My Name Is Rose* and a series of books called *Working Together*. Available from Dominie Press, 1361 Huntington Drive, Unit 7, Agincourt, Ontario, Canada M1S 3J1.

Urban Studies and Community Services Center. *Tell Me About It: Reading and Language Activities Around Multicultural Issues Based on an Oral History Approach.* (1986). By Azi Ellowitch. Available from Urban Studies and Community Services Center of LaSalle University, 5501 Wister Street, Philadelphia, PA 19144. (ERIC Document Reproduction Service No. ED 288 998)

Programs Focusing on Student-Published Materials

Detailed descriptions of programs in which adult ESL students write and publish their works are given in the following publications:

Cohen, C. (1983). Building multicultural and intergenerational networks through oral history. *Frontiers, 7*(1), 98-102.

Gillespie, M. (1990). *Many literacies: Modules for Training Adult Beginning Readers and Tutors.* Springfield, MA: Read/Write/Now Adult Learning Center. Available from CIE Publications Officer, 285 Hills House South, University of Massachusetts, Amherst, MA 01003. (ERIC Document Reproduction Service No. ED 324 463)

Listen to a new word: Publishing from the grassroots. (1989). [Special issue about student-produced materials.] *Focus on Basics, 2*(2).

Publishing an Anthology of Adult Student Writing: A Partnership for Literacy. (1985). Oxford, PA: Lincoln Intermediate Unit No. 12. (ERIC Document Reproduction Service Nos. ED 260 184 and ED 260 185)

Rawlston, S. (1988). My story: Refugee and immigrant students telling their personal histories. *TESOL in Action, 3*(1), 1-10. Available from *TESOL in Action*, c/o Linda Grant, The Language Institute, Education Extension, Georgia Institute of Technology, Atlanta, GA 30332.

Note

An earlier version of this chapter was published as an ERIC/NCLE Digest (ERIC Document Reproduction Service No. ED 317 096). I am grateful to Marilyn Gillespie, Rachel Martin, and Robert Thomas for their helpful comments on earlier versions.

References

Atwell, N. (1987). *In the middle: Writing, reading, and learning with adolescents*. Upper Montclair, NJ: Boynton/Cook.

Auerbach, E. (1989). Nontraditional materials for adult ESL. *TESOL Quarterly, 23*, 321-335.

Auerbach, E.R., & Burgess, D. (1985). The hidden curriculum of survival ESL. *TESOL Quarterly, 19*, 475-494.

Brod, S. (1990). *Recruiting and retaining language minority students in adult literacy programs*. Washington, DC: Center for Applied Linguistics, National Clearinghouse on Literacy Education. (ERIC Document Reproduction Service No. ED 321 621)

Calkins, L.M. (1983). *Lessons from a child: On the teaching and learning of writing*. Portsmouth, NH: Heinemann.

Calkins, L.M. (1986). *The art of teaching writing*. Portsmouth, NH: Heinemann.

Gaber-Katz, E., & Horsman, J. (1988). Is it her voice if she speaks their words? *Canadian Woman Studies, 9*(3 & 4), 117-120.

Gillespie, M. (1989). Research within reach: Participatory action research and the literacy classroom. *Focus on Basics, 2*(2), 8-9.

Graves, D.H. (1983). *Writing: Teachers and children at work*. Portsmouth, NH: Heinemann.

Hunter, C.S., & Harman, D. (1979). *Adult literacy in the United States*. New York: McGraw-Hill.

Martin, R. (Ed.). (1989, Spring). Listen to a new word: Publishing from the grassroots [Special issue]. *Focus on Basics, 2*(2), 1-4.

Murray, D.M. (1982). *Learning by teaching: Selected articles on writing and teaching*. Upper Montclair, NJ: Boynton/Cook.

Nishizaki, J. (1984). Multilingual voices. The National Writing Project newsletter. In *Publishing an anthology of adult student writing: A partnership for literacy* (pp. 45-46). [Oxford, PA: Lincoln Intermediate Unit No. 12.] (ERIC Document Reproduction Service No. ED 260 184)

Publishing an anthology of adult student writing: A partnership for literacy. (1985). Oxford, PA: Lincoln Intermediate Unit No. 12. (ERIC Document Reproduction Service No. ED 260 184 and ED 260 185)

Rawlston, S. (1988). My story: Refugee and immigrant students telling their personal histories. *TESOL in Action*, 3(1), 1-10.

Russell, D. (1985). Special projects in ESL—One class' story. *Connections: A Journal of Adult Literacy, 1*(1), 40-50. (ERIC Document Reproduction Service No. ED 260 227)

Wallerstein, N. (1983). *Language and culture in conflict.* Reading, MA: Addison-Wesley.

CHAPTER 5

The Freirean Approach to Adult Literacy Education

David Spener
University of Texas at Austin

Paulo Freire is an internationally known educator who has helped initiate, develop, and implement national literacy campaigns in a number of developing countries. Beginning in his native Brazil in the late 1950s, Freire's approach has been used in government-sponsored literacy programs in Chile, Mozambique, Angola, Guinea-Bissau, and Nicaragua. His writings on literacy and adult education gained worldwide recognition in the 1970s when Freire taught as a guest scholar at Harvard University and then went on to work at UNESCO in Geneva for several years. In addition to the government-run campaigns mentioned above, Freire's educational philosophy has inspired and guided literacy projects implemented by nongovernmental organizations in many countries and has had particular appeal to educators working with the poor and marginalized citizens of those countries. Among his most famous works are *A Pedagogy of the Oppressed* (1970), *Education for Critical Consciousness* (1973), and *The Politics of Education* (1985).

An Overview of the Freirean Approach

The Freirean approach to adult literacy education is not a method for reading and writing instruction per se but rather a fluid, philosophical approach to the organization and discussion of the thematic content of language study. It goes by a number of different names: problem posing (Auerbach & Wallerstein, 1987), psychosocial (Fargo, 1981; Hope, Timmel, & Hodzi, 1984), learner-centered (Añorve, 1989), liberatory (Facundo, 1984; Shor, 1980), and participatory (Jurmo, 1987), among others. Freire's approach has been called "deeply contextual" (Chacoff, 1989, p. 49), because in it, language study revolves around the discussion of issues drawn from the real-life experiences of adult learners.

Freire's approach emphasizes meaningful communication based on themes of emotional importance to learners. It is a content driven approach, in which the formal aspects of language play a secondary role to learners' conceptual development. Faigin (1985) points out the similarities among the educational approaches of Freire, John Dewey, and Bernard Mohan, and she maintains that Freire's approach owes much to the earlier work of John Dewey (1900), who rejected the abstract formalism of teaching in his day and argued in favor of the centrality of content in the study of language. She also sees the Freirean approach as having much in common with Mohan's "general framework for integrating language learning and content learning" (Faigin, 1985, p. 51), where students are language *users* first and language *learners* second (Mohan, 1984, 1986). Additionally, Wallerstein (1983) recognizes the similarities between the Freirean and the competency-based approaches to English as a second language (ESL) instruction in that both hold communication to be of central importance in language development and use, with the form of the language itself being of secondary importance. Finally, the Freirean approach shares the goals of learner centeredness and contextualization of literacy practices with the whole language approach described by Newman (1985), Goodman (1986), and Rigg and Kazemek (this volume).

Culture and Literacy Education

One manifestation of the sociocontextual orientation of the Freirean approach is its focus on the culture of students as the source of the thematic content for literacy classes. Here, it is important to understand the special definition of culture in Freirean terms. In *Education for Critical Consciousness*, Freire puts forth an "anthropological concept of culture" where culture is seen as "the addition made by men to a world they did not make, . . . the results of men's labor, of their efforts to create and re-create, the systematic acquisition of human experience" (1973, p. 46). Hemmendinger (1987) gives her "Freirean" definition of culture as "an interactive process of creating the world around oneself—participating in society and changing it through one's own contribution" (p. 60). Wallerstein adds that culture "includes how people labor, create, and make life choices" (1983, p. 5). In this view, culture is seen not as a static set of customs, religious beliefs, social attitudes, forms of address and attire, and foods, but rather a dynamic process of transformation and change laden with conflicts to resolve and choices to be made both individually and as a community.

It is Freire's position that reading and writing can have meaning only within this cultural context, and that the context itself must be analyzed and understood in order for literacy to be attained (Freire, 1973). Literacy, in turn, helps provide people with the tools to intervene actively in the shaping and transformation of their social reality by deepening their knowledge of that reality.

> To acquire literacy is more than to psychologically and mechanically dominate reading and writing techniques. It is to dominate those techniques in terms of consciousness; to understand what one reads and to write what one understands; it is to communicate graphically. (Freire, 1973, p. 48)

In advocating the whole language approach, Newman (1985) refers to the same idea of literacy as a tool for gaining knowledge:

> We begin to see reading and writing . . . as a means by which students can take an active part in their own learning. . . . knowledge isn't something which exists separate from people; people are actively engaged in creating what they know or understand. . . . as students write and read they reshape their view of the world and extend their ability to think about it. (p. 2)

Liberatory Education

For Freire, however, education and knowledge have no value in and of themselves. Education has value only insofar as it helps people to liberate themselves from the social conditions that oppress them, hence the term *liberatory education*. Freire views illiteracy not as the cause of an individual's oppression, but rather as a result and symptom of it. According to Freire (1985), illiteracy is "one of the concrete expressions of an unjust social reality . . . not a strictly linguistic or exclusively pedagogical or methodological problem. It is political" (p. 10). In an analysis of various views on learner participation in adult literacy education, Jurmo (1989) summarizes the following view of advocates of social change.

> Advocates of social change claim that, to understand [the problems faced by most uneducated adults], we must study the historical conditions that shape an illiterate adult's life. In the case of a large segment of the adult nonreaders in the United

States, life has been characterized by poor physical conditions, poor-quality education, inferior social status, and a lack of economic and political power.

Supporters of the social-change analysis argue that *it is not a coincidence that many non-readers live in oppressive conditions* [emphasis added]. Their illiteracy is a direct result of the conditions, and there is little chance that the cycle of illiteracy within oppressed populations will be broken unless the conditions are eliminated. *It is the job of adult education to enable learners to participate actively in changing those conditions* [emphasis added]. (p. 22)

Freire himself argues:

This pedagogy makes oppression and its causes objects of reflection by the oppressed, and from that reflection will come their necessary engagement in the struggle for their liberation. . . . In order for the oppressed to be able to wage the struggle for their liberation, they must perceive the reality of oppression not as a closed world from which there is no exit, but as a limiting situation which they can transform. (Freire, 1970, pp. 33-34)

Freire sees the educational process as an opportunity for illiterate and semiliterate students to practice and experience the principles of democracy and self-determination for the first time in their lives. He says that the approach used should encourage learners to make decisions and take action to improve their lives. It should not be surprising, then, that the institutions most likely to espouse Freire's educational philosophy to literacy instruction see themselves as agents of social change. In the United States and in other countries not in situations of revolutionary change, nongovernmental organizations such as trade unions and community-based organizations have been the most likely to employ Freire's nonformal approach. The Association for Community Based Education's definition of a community-based organization (CBO) gives an indication of why CBOs are likely adherents to the Freirean approach:

[CBOs are] groups set up to serve a given geographical area and constituency, usually urban or rural poverty communities and the educationally, economically and socially disadvantaged. They are formed by their constituencies—including . . . ethnic, racial, and cultural minorities—to meet specific needs that exist within the community. . . . They often link education to community development activities. Their methodological approaches are nontraditional, to meet the needs of those whom traditional education has failed, and learner centered, focused on helping people meet objectives they themselves set in response to their own needs. (Association for Community Based Education, n.d., pp. 2-3)

Freire's Early Brazilian Experience

In Brazil in the early 1960s, Freire worked with a team of anthropologists, educators, and students to develop a program of initial literacy instruction in Portuguese for rural peasants and villagers. The team began its work with an extended period of ethnographic research in the communities where the program was to be implemented. Members of the literacy team spent time in those communities, participating in informal conversations with residents, observing their culture, experiencing their lifestyle, and listening to their life stories. One of the purposes was to research the vocabulary of the communities, looking for recurring words and themes to be included in materials for the literacy program. From this research into the lifestyle, life stories, and vocabulary of the communities, Freire's teams developed lists of words and expressions that seemed to be of recurring importance in the conversations they had with residents. From among these words, planners chose *generative words,* words that would later be used as keys to helping students develop the basic decoding and encoding skills for reading and writing:

> [words] whose syllabic elements offer, through recombination, the creation of new words. Teaching men how to read and write a syllabic language like Portuguese means showing them how to grasp critically the way its words are formed, so that they themselves can carry out the creative play of combinations. Fifteen or eighteen words seemed sufficient to present the basic phonemes of the Portuguese language. (Freire, 1973, p. 49)

It was not enough, however, that these generative words were phonemically rich in terms of the syllables they could generate through manipulation and recombination. These words had to hold special meaning and be of special emotional importance to participants in the literacy program. In this way, Freire's approach coincides with the literacy method used by Sylvia Ashton-Warner in teaching Maori children to read in New Zealand. Ashton-Warner maintained that the first words children learned to read should be the words that they themselves had spoken and decided to learn to read (Ashton-Warner, 1963).

Based on the themes identified in their ethnographic research, Freire and his team had an artist draw ten scenes from the rural communities to be used to generate discussion in the literacy classes. The situations represented in each drawing contained conflicts within the culture of the community for students to recognize, analyze, and attempt to resolve as a group. The situations were familiar and emotionally laden to stimulate active debate and discussion on themes that learners already knew directly. The generative words culled from the field vocabulary lists compiled in the research phase of the literacy campaign could be found embedded in these codifications, such that they likely would be spoken by group members as they analyzed the scenes and discussed the key conflicts they depicted.

Exercises were then developed using discovery cards, based on the generative words described above. Each discovery card contained the breakdown of a generative word into its component syllables, giving learners the opportunity to recombine syllables to form other words in their vocabulary (Freire, 1973). Use of the discovery card method was in keeping with established syllabary techniques frequently used to teach word attack skills in phonetically and orthographically regular languages such as Spanish and Portuguese. (See Fauteux & Alamo, 1990, and Gudschinsky, 1976).

The effect of combining the discussion of picture codes with syllabary exercises based on the vocabulary generated by the pictures was to link metaphorically observed reality with spoken, and then written, language. First, learners decoded the pictures using spoken language as their tool. Next, they saw their spoken words encoded by the teacher in the form of writing, which they then decoded again into their component syllables. Finally, using the discovery cards, they encoded once more, recombining raw syllables to form new words.

Dialogue and Problem Posing in Freirean Literacy Classes

The essence of the Freirean approach lies deeper than indicated by the above description of his early work in literacy in Brazil. It lies rather in the teacher-student and student-student relationships established in the educational setting and in the form of dialogue and inquiry that occurs. In "reading the world" as well as in "reading the word," exponents of the Freirean approach advocate a teacher-student relationship of collaboration and dialogue between equals (Facundo, 1984; Faigin, 1985; Freire, 1970, 1973; Noble, 1983; Shor, 1980; Wallerstein, 1983). This relationship should be one where both teacher and student play the role of active subjects in the educational process.

The lecture format, where the teacher talks and the students passively receive information, is replaced by the "culture circle," where teachers and students face one another and discuss issues of concern to their own lives (Freire, 1970, 1973). Freirean educators vehemently reject what Freire has termed "the banking concept of education":

> [Teachers attempt] to intercede "on students' behalf" by presenting them with a humanitarian aid package that includes this unstated proviso: Instead of using the reality of existence and your innate capacity to construct knowledge and language, we (the knowing teachers) will invent "reality" in the classroom and *give* "knowledge of language" to you as deposits of information. (Graman, 1988, p. 434)

They hold instead:

> Teachers and students *together* search for the answers to the questions: What are the objective forces in the world that shape our consciousness and our character? Why are things like they are? What oppresses us and how can we change it? (Faigin, 1985, p. 7)

In addition to dialogue, another key element in the Freirean approach is that of problem posing. Problem posing is probably the most misunderstood of terms associated with Freire, perhaps due to the negative connotations given to the word problem and to the frequent discussion of problem-solving skills in educational circles. Wallerstein (1983) defines problem posing as a tool for developing critical thinking skills that consists of "an inductive questioning process that structures dialogue in the classroom. Teachers formulate questions to encourage students to make their own conclusions about society's values and pressures" (p. 17).

In relation to the codifications of reality, or pictures, used by Freire in the Brazilian program, the teacher asks open-ended questions about the pictures being discussed, asking students to describe what they see, what relationships exist among the different people and objects in the picture, and how they feel about what they see. Ultimately, students are asked to identify the problem illustrated and to propose solutions to the problem (Freire, 1973; Wallerstein, 1983). In the process, students should gain new insights into the limitations to and the possibilities for their freedom and advancement in society as they "extraordinarily reexperience the ordinary" (Shor, 1980). This consciousness-raising process has been called "concientizicão" by Freire, sometimes translated as "conscienticization" in English. (See, e.g., Auerbach, 1992).

Graman (1988) and Fargo (1981) see the practice of problem posing or problematizing reality as part of creating the "teachable moment" in the classroom. Graman relates problem posing and the resolution of conflict in the educational process to Piaget's theories of cognitive development:

> Piaget emphasized the importance of experiencing states of disequilibrium and of reequilibrium in order to advance intellectual development, for such anxiety, disequilibrium, or conflict is part of the struggle for knowledge that all learners must experience in order to understand or make that knowledge their own. . . . Students build critical knowledge and the language to express it . . . through engaging in "problematizing" reality—that is, learners must identify problems and come to recognize and understand the significance of those problems in relation to their own lives and the lives of others. (Graman, 1988, pp. 5-6)

Auerbach and Burgess (1985) distinguish between *problem posing* in the Freirean approach and the problem solving orientation of other literacy and basic education approaches. Problem posing, they say, gives learners the chance to identify their own set of problems and to seek their own solutions. Problem solving, on the other hand, identifies problems for them a priori and gives them the knowledge to solve those problems:

Problem solving often takes the form of chunking reality into competencies corresponding to specific skills judged necessary for successful functioning in American society. . . . By contrast, [in] a problem-posing view of education . . . the teacher's role is not to transmit knowledge but to engage students in their own education by inviting them to enter into the process of thinking critically about their reality. (Auerbach & Burgess, 1985, p. 491)

Reinventing Freire for Literacy in English as a Second Language

The Freirean approach, like the counseling-learning approach developed by Father Charles Curran (1976), has been reinvented and applied ex post facto to second-language learning contexts. ESL literacy teachers in the United States and Canada have attempted to apply Freire's general approach using those special ESL teaching methods and techniques they find compatible with it. Some familiar ESL methods and techniques that have been used by Freirean practitioners have included language experience stories, oral histories, Total Physical Response, jazz chants, strip stories and sentences, cloze dictations, paired reading, and dialogue journal writing.

Two important difficulties with adapting the Freirean approach to ESL literacy are readily apparent. First, the approach assumes that learners are highly knowledgeable about the culture in which they live and that they are expert speakers of the language that they are learning to read and write. For language minorities learning English in countries where English is the majority language, neither of these conditions applies. How, then, can an approach building upon the oral base of the learner's language be used when the base may not yet exist in the target language?

Second, the English language's spelling and syllabic structures do not lend themselves to the syllabary method originally used by Freire in Spanish and Portuguese. How, then, can generative words be used to build word-attack skills in reading and writing? Some practitioners using a Freirean approach with native speakers of English dialects as well as with minority language adults have used a whole word and word family method, where learners memorize the spelling of each new vocabulary word and place it in a list with other words on the basis of similar morphological structure or related meaning. The word "American," for example, might appear in two different word lists: one with words such as "African," "Dominican," and "Canadian," and another with words suggested by students, such as "apple pie," "Statue of Liberty," and "rich" (R.L. Añorve, personal communication, October 10, 1988). Other practitioners (such as those at the Bronx Educational Services in New York City, for example) adapt the use of generative words to the phonics method of reading instruction, where students learn the spelling patterns of English in order to sound out new words they need to read and write. Still others have abandoned the generative words method altogether in favor of other whole language techniques developed for English.

Many professional and volunteer ESL teachers in the English-speaking countries have developed adaptations of the Freirean approach for their ESL programs. Models for ESL literacy using re-inventions of the Freirean approach include the model for ESL development for groups of adults from different native-language backgrounds described by Nina Wallerstein in her book *Language and Culture in Conflict* (1983); the approach taken by Anna Hemmendinger (1987) in working with Hmong refugees in Canada; and a bilingual model developed by Spener (1991) for use in classes of Central American refugees in Washington, DC.

Wallerstein

Nina Wallerstein's Freirean model for ESL is detailed in her book *Language and Culture in Conflict* (1983). Of the three models discussed here, hers is the most similar to Freire's work in Brazil. She describes her approach as occurring in three stages—listening, dialogue, and action. She notes that ESL teachers and students come from different cultural, linguistic, and economic backgrounds that must be recognized for their differences and their validity. As a result, teachers must make special efforts to get to know the realities faced by students in their personal lives and communities either through cohabitation (preferred) or observation (the next best alternative). She recommends that teachers visit the homes of their students as an invited guest to learn firsthand about their lives and families. To learn about the cultural attributes of the students, a teacher should attempt to be present as an observer at times of 1) cultural transmission from the older generation to the younger (social rites and child rearing practices); 2) cultural preservation (festivals and historic celebrations in the immigrant/language minority neighborhoods); and 3) cultural disruption (asking students about their immigration to the host country and to compare their lives in the home country with their lives in the host country). The teacher should also become familiar with the neighborhoods in which the students live, walking in them alone or with her students, taking photographs to discuss, or bringing realia from the neighborhoods back to class. In class, teachers should observe student-student interactions, their body language, and actions because these usually reveal students' priorities and problems. To facilitate validation of the students' culture(s), the teacher should also invite students to share objects from their culture with others in class, as well as create curriculum flowing from the students' everyday cultural activities: "Cross-cultural understanding comes in what we as teachers observe, transform into curriculum, and then receive in feedback from our students" (p. 15).

Dialogue for Wallerstein signifies a process in which "students initiate discussions, lessons, and activities to fulfill their educational needs" (p. 15).

> In an ABE/ESL class, this dialogue assumes many forms. In *curriculum* content, students introduce their personal backgrounds, their needs for education, their cultural differences with each other and with Anglo-America, and the problems they confront daily. In *classroom dynamics*, students participate in discussion circles, divide into small groups or pairs for structured peer teaching, or learn directly from the teacher. In *attitudes*, students and teachers communicate as co-learners. (p. 15)

Wallerstein's use of codifications as the basis for problem posing discussions is similar to Freire's except that the media she uses are more diverse; in addition to pictures, they include oral histories, short stories, poems, skits, songs, comics, and puppet shows. She must also account for her students' limited proficiency in English as the codifications are discussed orally. She recommends that problem posing skills be built "concretely in an English class, with teachers starting at the descriptive level to reinforce language. In the first days of class, students can learn the question words: who, what, where, why, when and how, and exchange information from the very start" (p. 19). Other beginner techniques she recommends are writing simple autobiographies, using flash cards to introduce new vocabulary and structures, Total Physical Response activities, lessons for building the vocabulary for emotions, and a "microwave" method for teaching dialogue in which one grammatical structure is introduced at a time and is modeled with puppets.

Hemmendinger

Anna Hemmendinger developed an adaptation of the Freirean approach for ESL literacy classes with Laotian Hmong refugees in Ontario (Hemmendinger, 1987). Working with the Hmong presented special problems in implementing a Freirean ESL model. First, the Hmong come from a nonliterate culture where their mother tongue has only recently been written, and literacy is not required to participate in the native culture. Second, Hemmendinger found that the Hmong were accustomed to, and in fact seemed to favor, the "banking education" model with an authoritarian teacher directing them. This, she says, caused her initially to follow a "transitionary" approach, using drill and memorization techniques with some more participatory elements "sneaked-in" (pp. 51-52).

Hemmendinger was committed to a Freirean approach in spite of these obstacles and based her commitment on her views of the relationship between language and culture.

> Language is the primary vehicle through which people participate in or have access to culture. Thus, as the learners begin to pose problems about their lives, their questioning and desire to participate in the wider society creates a motivation for second language learning. (p. 60)

Hemmendinger based her model on examination, with the students, of themes from their Hmong culture in Laos, from the dominant culture in Canada, and from their transposed Hmong culture in Canada. She described the Hmong's Laotian culture as their past culture that had become fossilized at the moment of their emigration. This culture she frequently found codified in the elaborate embroideries sewn by the Hmong women, which depicted scenes from Laos. Some elements of the Hmong's past culture, such as the practice of polygamy, were legally prohibited in Canada. The dominant culture was the one in which the majority of Canadians participated, and the transposed culture consisted of a mixture of Laotian and Canadian elements.

> Unlike the static, past culture, the transposed culture is constantly changing according to how much people remember of the past, or how well they can re-create the past environment,

e.g., how much their transposed culture is moderated by the new dominant culture. (p. 28)

Hemmendinger actually developed two models for teaching her ESL classes. Both models involved using a bilingual aide in class to facilitate dialogue on the cultural themes and problems that generated the curriculum. In her first model, problem posing flowed from the sharing of cultural information, whereas in the second, the sharing of cultural information resulted from a problem under discussion in the classroom. She found many cultural themes and problems within the classroom itself. For example, she once found a student closely examining all the potted plants in the class. When Hemmendinger, through the bilingual aide, inquired as to why he was interested in the plants, she learned that the student was a practitioner of Hmong herbal medicine. This led to a discussion of Hmong health and medicinal practices compared with those practiced by the dominant culture in Canada and of problems that students were having as they confronted the Canadian health care system. The educational model she developed for problematizing cultural themes was as follows:

1. Listen and identify the theme.
2. Dialogue and share customs in the past/transposed culture.
3. Discuss customs in the dominant culture.
4. Compare and contrast customs in the dominant and transposed cultures.
5. Pose problems in the dominant culture.
6. Raise related themes, problems, and possible solutions.
7. Discuss alternate solutions.
8. Design and implement language learning activities.

In another instance, Hemmendinger came to class and found her students involved in an animated discussion in the back of the room. Again working with the help of her bilingual aide, she discovered that a number of students had been "ripped-off" working for a worm farmer at night. Hemmendinger abandoned her lesson plan for the day to write language experience stories and related exercises about the incident with the students in both Hmong and English. The language experience stories were then used as codifications upon which further discussion took place. The model Hemmendinger elaborated for this sort of class situation was as follows:

1. Raise the problem.

2. Design and practice language learning exercises.

3. Dialogue about the situation.

4. Discuss possible solutions to the problem.

5. Take action to solve the problem.

6. Analyze the same situation in the transposed culture.

7. Propose alternate solutions.

8. Raise additional themes to discuss.

The stages of the educational process that Hemmendinger proposes in her models vary from those proposed by Wallerstein. For Hemmendinger, the problem in problem posing is not always a social problem, but one found in the educational process itself. For her, identifying a problem may consist of "identifying gaps in skills or knowledge needed to attain goals." "Action" may not necessarily be community action for social change, but may be "participating in a learning process based on personal experience and community need" in the classroom itself (p. 53). In order to fill the gaps in skills or knowledge that students identified as blocking the attainment of their goals, Hemmendinger incorporated elements of functional and competency-based literacy approaches into her teaching. Other Freirean practitioners (Auerbach & Burgess, 1985; Graman, 1988) might see this as inconsistent with Freire's general approach.

Hemmendinger cautions that there are problems with the Freirean approach in the ESL classroom. The most notable she says, is that a great deal of flexibility and effort is required on the part of the teacher to incorporate cultural themes and real-life problems that students bring to class into the ESL curriculum. Nonetheless, she remains an adherent to the Freirean approach:

> Problem posing . . . is at variance with Hmong traditional values and practices. However, through introducing it with cultural sharing as described in the two models, the Hmong not only engaged in problem posing in the class but also applied it to their lives outside of class. (p. 82)

Spener

Working with Spanish-speaking Central American refugee families in apartment-based ESL classes in Washington, DC, I attempted to adapt the Freirean approach by "problematizing" the process of learning English (Spener, 1990a, 1990b, 1991). The students in the Spanish Education Center's *Inglés en su Casa* (English at Home) program were mainly peasants and workers from Guatemala and El Salvador who spoke little or no English and whose literacy skills in Spanish had either never been developed or had atrophied since they left school. Many students were recent arrivals to the United States and lived and worked in communities with large numbers of Spanish-speaking residents, where they could meet most of their routine survival needs without much English. Some had studied English in formal classes but had dropped out early either because their lack of literacy in Spanish proved a barrier to their understanding, or because work schedules, family responsibilities, high transportation costs, and unsafe night streets deterred their regular attendance.

In *Inglés en su Casa,* all teachers were bilingual and students all spoke Spanish, which facilitated the kind of dialogue and problem posing described by Hemmendinger above. Notwithstanding this advantage, I encountered two problems in applying a Freirean approach in this adult ESL literacy program. First, in a Freirean approach, the thematic content of language learning typically consists of the personal and social problems encountered by learners in their communities. The *Inglés en su Casa* students had not invited teachers into their homes to discuss these issues—they had invited them to teach them English as quickly and as painlessly as possible. In fact, in a home setting with other family members present, students were perhaps even less willing to discuss these issues than they would have been in a formal classroom setting. Second, the discussion of community and personal issues, in terms of language domains and choice, was most naturally carried out in Spanish—it was the in-group language to be used for communicating about issues of importance to the Spanish-speaking community. English was seen as a tool for communicating with members of the English-speaking community from which the Spanish-speaking ESL students still felt separate. It soon became clear to me that the "teachable moment" for English would come when the problems posed in the ESL class were integral and not simply instrumental to the students' self-defined needs to speak, read, and write in English in their day-to-day lives.

I attempted to incorporate elements of dialogue and problem posing into both the curriculum and the class structure. For each group I worked with, I facilitated an initial workshop to set up the agenda for studying English. The workshops were conducted in Spanish and English and involved a self-directed needs assessment of the group, by the group. Each participant in the initial workshop was asked to answer the following questions (in Spanish):

Where and with whom do you currently use English?

Where and with whom do you urgently need to use English?

What are the daily situations with which you have the most trouble because you don't know enough English?

Each person's answer was recorded in Spanish and English next to their name on a sheet of butcher-block paper taped to the wall. When everyone's responses were received, the group was asked to identify responses that appeared for more than one question. For each situation identified in this way, the group was then asked to consider and reach a consensus on the questions, *How many people here experience this situation currently? Is it worth spending time studying it in class? Why do you think so? Why not?* Typical situations chosen by groups included communicating with supervisors at work, communicating with school personnel, and communicating with pharmacists, doctors, and health workers.

I used these study agendas to write statements of performance-based language competencies for students to master in each situation on their agenda. I wrote these competency statements in Spanish and English and brought them back to class for students to discuss, reject, modify, or approve. I then designed specific language acquisition activities for spoken and written English based on the competencies chosen by a given group of learners. Periodic group discussions took place where students evaluated their mastery of their competency goals, added new competencies for given situations, and created new study agendas upon completion of the old ones.

I attempted to integrate dialogue and problem posing on a regular basis into three parts of each class period. First was the daily "check-in," when students were asked to share with the class how they were feeling and one success and one difficulty they had experienced outside class during the week. Questions were asked of each student in English by a rotating facilitator from the group, and each student was encouraged to respond using as much English as they could. Other students and the facilitator would help with new vocabulary and discuss possible solutions to difficulties students were experiencing. Responses, new vocabulary, and possible solutions to problems were recorded on newsprint for students to copy and later use to write a weekly class newsletter for student reading practice that included cloze exercises and dictation practice.

Another time when dialogue regularly took place in class was during "inquietudes" ("questions and concerns"), when students brought in questions about English vocabulary they had seen or heard in the community between classes but had not understood. I used a "transitional spelling" technique described by Tomás Kalmar (1983). This technique involved writing down English words heard by students as if those words were Spanish, and then writing them a second time using the real spelling in English. This gave me extra help in deciphering what were often unintelligible words and phrases, and also seemed to reinforce the link between spoken and written language in the minds of the students. An example of the use of this technique was "guiradajir" (Get outta here!) shouted at one student as she witnessed what appeared to be a drug transaction between two men on a street corner. Material generated from inquietudes was recycled into the reading and writing curriculum in much the same way as that from check-in.

The third time when dialogue and problem posing occurred in class was in a group evaluation at the end of each class. Conducted in English and Spanish, this was a brief criticism/self-criticism session of that class and the group's progress toward attaining the goals on its agenda. Students and teachers were asked to answer these questions as concretely as possible:

What were the weak points of this class?

What were the strong points?

What could the teacher do better?

What could the students do better?

What other changes could we make to improve the way the class is conducted?

As in the check-in and inquietudes described above, material from the group evaluation discussion found its way back into the literacy curriculum through the class newsletter and other language acquisition activities. Following the group evaluation discussion, students would be given time to write in dialogue journals. This provided a private, one-to-one vehicle for dialogue and individual reading and writing development, and an additional means to gain insights into the lives and culture of students. (See Spener, 1991, for a description.)

Rethinking Freire: Theoretical Critiques and Pragmatic Considerations

In recent years, both research on literacy as a sociocultural and cognitive phenomenon and the practical experiences of teachers and students have led to revisions of the "classical" Freirean approach to literacy. Theoreticians have begun to question Freire's emphasis on the importance of literacy to the liberation of society's poor. Research into the ethnography of literacy has begun to challenge what Brian Street (1984) has referred to as the "Great Divide ideology" that previously held sway. Street and others (Gundlach, Farr, & Cook-Gumperz, in press; Heath, 1983; Reder, 1990) have come to reject the "autonomous view" of literacy that maintains that there is a "Great Divide" separating literate people from illiterate people.

> According to this theory, "illiterates" are fundamentally separate from literates. For individuals this is taken to mean that ways of thinking, cognitive abilities, facility in logic, abstraction, and higher order mental operations are all integrally related to the achievement of literacy. The corollary is that illiterates are presumed to lack all of these qualities, to be able to think less abstractly, to be more embedded, less critical, less able to reflect upon the nature of the language they use or the sources of their political oppression. It appears obvious, then, that illiterates should be made literate in order to give them all of these characteristics and to "free" them from the oppression and "ignorance" associated with their lack of literacy skills. (Street, 1990, p. 9)

There is some irony in this critique of Freire, since his has been one of the strongest voices propounding the idea that illiteracy is more likely to be caused by poverty than to cause it. Still, it is true that Freire has forcefully stated that he believes that the development of literacy and a critical consciousness about social reality do go hand-in-hand, and that both are tools that the world's poor require to liberate themselves from their oppression. Street seems to accuse Freire of overselling the benefits of literacy, much as reading theorist Frank Smith has accused the educational and political establishments of doing, although they do so from a very different political position. It should be pointed out, however, that this critique is not of the Freirean approach per se, but rather of the claim that following it will lead to social change initiated by neo-literates.

In *Making Meaning, Making Change: Participatory Curriculum Development for Adult ESL Literacy* (1992), Elsa Auerbach summarizes some of the revisions practitioners have made of both Freire's original approach and its reinventions in ESL:

> As the body of Freire-inspired practice grows, there have been inevitable refinements, reformulations, and challenges to both the form and content of Freire's ideas. Key among these is expansion of the learners' role in the curriculum development process; specifically, where Freire suggested that the educator undertake a period of investigation and identification of themes before instruction begins, others have moved toward a process of identifying themes through dialogue with participants, as part of the instructional process. In addition, rather than focusing on a single method (moving from code to dialogue to generative word to syllabification to creating new words and moving toward action), others have expanded the range of tools and processes for exploring issues, with student involvement in the production of material. Further, many have questioned the notion that the teacher's role is to facilitate conscienticization and analytical thinking because it implies that the teacher has a more developed understanding than the students. (Auerbach, 1992, p. 18)

An integral concept to these revisions of Freirean practice is the notion of the *emergent curriculum* (Auerbach, 1992). ESL and native language literacy teachers practicing in large urban centers in the United States have found it impractical, if not impossible, to engage in the sort of Phase I field investigation of learner themes as practiced by Freire in Brazil. First of all, most adult literacy instructors work part time, are underpaid, and do not have the paid time to conduct such thorough investigations before entering the classroom. Secondly, the students in adult ESL and native language literacy classes do not live in integrated, stable communities where such investigations could be carried out. Students in a single class may represent a variety of national, cultural, and linguistic backgrounds and may live in quite dispersed locations throughout a given metropolitan area.

The only thing that immediately links them together as a community is their participation in the literacy class. Hence, the exploration of community cultural themes can emerge from interactions in class only as the "community" constitutes and reconstitutes itself over time.

These and similar collisions with "real life" have also brought about changes in the inductive questioning process based on teacher-made codes advocated by Wallerstein (1983). Auerbach (1992) and Nash, Cason, Gomez-Sanford, McGrail, & Rhum (1992) have described how the problem posing process often does not move in the stepwise, linear fashion they had once anticipated. In an emergent curriculum, the teacher does not plan a sequenced set of discussions based on picture codes that then generate literacy lessons. Codes, when used, must be created as themes emerge in the class-community, often in collaboration with the students themselves. (One practice, for example, is for students to engage in collective drawings illustrating a problem or an experience they share in common and then discuss and write about it.) Supplementing codes is the notion of tools that can be used to foment class discussion of themes. Tools used in class can be laid out along a continuum from most teacher-controlled (published texts, preselected photos from magazines) to those jointly controlled by teacher and students (collaboratively produced materials such as a class newsletter) to most student-controlled (class skits, family histories) (Auerbach, 1992).

Educators worldwide have been drawn to the Freirean approach because of its political dimension: The possibility that as economically marginalized adults become more literate and aware of the social forces at work in society, they will organize themselves to transform the social structures that keep them marginalized. For Freire and those whose work he has inspired, the *raison d'etre* for the Freirean approach has been that it leads to learners taking action for social change (liberation) in their communities. In many developing nations, the approach has been linked to peasant struggles for land reform, struggles to unionize workplaces, and struggles of indigenous peoples to defend their rights to their land and way of life. With immigrants and refugees in literacy and ESL classes in the United States, it is perhaps less likely that actions taken by students will be so dramatic, particularly when students are still only getting their bearings in the new country. Does this mean that the Freirean approach should, by its own standards, be judged as a failure with regard to ESL and minority language literacy education in the United States?

Staff of the University of Massachusetts Family Literacy Project posed this question and in answering it have proposed that the Freirean conception of action be reformulated so that it includes educational outcomes that may not be directly linked to organized, group struggles for social change. They found that action-outcomes in their students' lives run along a continuum from those at the personal and individual level to those at the collective and societal level. Auerbach (1992) gives specific examples: a discussion among women students of their experiences as overworked mothers and wives with no time for personal enjoyment, leading to one of the women joining a women's softball team; concern in class with issues of bilingualism, family/cultural life, and the schooling of children, leading one student to join a Latino parents advocacy group; students convening a public reading of works they had written in class; class activities and discussions helping individual parents regain lost self-esteem as they became less dependent upon their children for accomplishing tasks requiring English and more confident of the value of preserving their own cultural and linguistic heritage; learning about a threat to the funding of adult education programs in the Massachusetts state budget, leading a group of students to meet with state representatives to demand that funds be released.

> We had to realize that group actions don't fall from the sky, with whole groups deciding to do something at once, but rather they often start with one or two people taking the initiative, having a success which others hear about and begin to network around. With these realizations in mind, we moved toward an expanded concept of action. (Auerbach, 1992, pp. 105-106)

These revisions of Freire by a group of local practitioners seem to speak directly to the critique of Freire by Street (1990), cited above, and bring the Freirean approach more definitively out of the Great Divide paradigm. The revisions also may help literacy educators avoid becoming disheartened when their teaching does not seem to engender an increase in readily observable social activism on the part of their students.

References

Añorve, R.L. (1989). Community-based literacy educators: Experts and catalysts for change. *New Directions for Continuing Education, 42*, 35-42.

Ashton-Warner, S. (1963). *Teacher*. New York: Simon and Schuster.

Association for Community Based Education. (n.d.). *A project to strengthen community-based adult literacy programs.* [Funding proposal]. Washington, DC: Association for Community Based Education.

Auerbach, E.R. (1992). *Making meaning, making change: Participatory curriculum development for adult ESL literacy*. McHenry, IL and Washington, DC: Delta Systems and Center for Applied Linguistics.

Auerbach, E.R., & Burgess, D. (1985). The hidden curriculum of survival ESL. *TESOL Quarterly, 10*, 475-495.

Auerbach, E.R., & Wallerstein, N. (1987). *ESL for action: Problem-posing at work*. Reading, MA: Addison-Wesley.

Chacoff, A. (1989). *(Bi)literacy and empowerment: Education for indigenous groups in Brazil.* (Working Papers in Educational Linguistics). Philadelphia: University of Pennsylvania, Language Education Division.

Curran, C.A. (1976). *Counseling-learning in second language*. East Dubuque, IL: Counseling-Learning Publications.

Dewey, J. (1900). *The school and society*. Chicago: University of Chicago Press.

Facundo, B. (1984). *Issues for an evaluation of Freire-inspired programs in the United States and Puerto Rico*. Reston, VA: Latino Institute. (ERIC Document Reproduction Service No. ED 243 998)

Faigin, S. (1985). *Basic ESL literacy from a Freirean perspective: A curriculum unit for farmworker education*. Major essay for the degree of Master of Education, University of British Columbia, Vancouver. (ERIC Document Reproduction Service No. ED 274 196)

Fargo, G.A. (1981). *The power of literacy applied to traditional birth attendants, Saulteaux-Cree Indians and Hawaiian children.* Paper presented at the 48th annual meeting of the Claremont

Reading Conference, Claremont, CA. (ERIC Document Reproduction Service No. ED 201 967)

Fauteux, D., & Alamo, M. (1990). *Palabras de lucha y alegría* [*Words of struggle and joy*]. Syracuse, NY: New Readers Press.

Freire, P. (1970). *Pedagogy of the oppressed*. New York: Continuum.

Freire, P. (1973). *Education for critical consciousness*. New York: Seabury.

Freire, P. (1985). *The politics of education*. New York: Bergin and Garvey.

Goodman, K. (1986). *What's whole in whole language?* Portsmouth, NH: Heinemann.

Graman, T. (1988). Education for humanization: Applying Paulo Freire's pedagogy to learning a second language. *Harvard Educational Review, 58,* 433-448.

Gudschinsky, S.C. (1976). *Handbook of literacy*. Dallas: Summer Institute of Linguistics.

Gundlach, R., Farr, M., & Cook-Gumperz, J. (in press). Writing and reading in the community. In A. Dyson (Ed.), *Writing and reading: Collaboration in the classroom*. Urbana, IL: National Council of Teachers of English.

Heath, S.B. (1983). *Ways with words*. Cambridge: Cambridge University Press.

Hemmendinger, A. (1987). *Two models for using problem-posing and cultural sharing in teaching the Hmong English as a second language and first language literacy*. Unpublished master's thesis, St. Francis Xavier University, Antigonish, Nova Scotia.

Hope, A., Timmel S., & Hodzi, C. (1984). *Training for transformation* (Vols. 1-3). Harare, Zimbabwe: Mambo.

Jurmo, P. (1987). *Learner participation practices in adult literacy efforts in the United States*. Unpublished doctoral dissertation, University of Massachusetts, Amherst. (ERIC Document Reproduction Service No. ED 317 091)

Jurmo, P. (1989). The case for participatory literacy education. In A. Fingeret & P. Jurmo (Eds.), *Participatory literacy education* (pp. 17-34). San Francisco: Jossey-Bass.

Kalmar, T.M. (1983). *The voice of Fulano: Working papers from a bilingual literacy campaign*. Cambridge, MA: Schenkman.

Mohan, B.A. (1984, March). *A general framework for integrating language learning and content learning*. Paper presented at the convention of Teachers of English to Speakers of Other Languages, Houston, TX.

Mohan, B.A. (1986). *Language and content*. Reading, MA: Addison-Wesley.

Nash, A., Cason, A., Gomez-Sanford, R., McGrail, L., & Rhum, M. (1992). *Talking shop: A curriculum sourcebook for participatory adult ESL*. McHenry, IL and Washington, DC: Delta Systems and Center for Applied Linguistics.

Newman, J. (Ed.). (1985). *Whole language: Theory in use*. Portsmouth, NH: Heinemann.

Noble, P. (1983). *Formation of Freirean facilitators*. Chicago: Latino Institute. (ERIC Document Reproduction Service No. ED 256 845)

Reder, S. (1990, March). *Literacy across languages and cultures: The issue addressed in terms of society and its institutions: An overview*. Paper presented at the Gutenberg Conference, Albany, NY.

Shor, I. (1980). *Critical teaching and everyday life*. Chicago: University of Chicago Press.

Spener, D. (1990a). *Setting an agenda for study in home-based ESL classes with native speakers of Spanish*. Unpublished manuscript. (ERIC Document Reproduction Service No. ED 318 301)

Spener, D. (1990b). *Suggested structure for meetings of home-based ESL classes for native speakers of Spanish*. Unpublished manuscript. (ERIC Document Reproduction Service No. ED 318 300)

Spener, D. (1991). Getting started: Dialogue journal writing with semiliterate adult ESL students. In J.K. Peyton & J. Staton (Eds.), *Writing our lives: Reflections on dialogue journal writing with adults learning English* (pp. 67-77). Englewood Cliffs, NJ: Regents/Prentice Hall and Center for Applied Linguistics.

Street, B.V. (1984). *Literacy in theory and practice*. New York: Cambridge University Press.

Street, B.V. (1990). Putting literacies on the political agenda. *Open Letter: Australian Journal for Adult Literacy Research and Practice, 1*, 5-15.

Wallerstein, N. (1983). *Language and culture in conflict: Problem-posing in the ESL classroom*. Reading, MA: Addison-Wesley.

Language in Education: Theory and Practice

The **Educational Resources Information Center (ERIC)**, which is supported by the Office of Educational Research and Improvement of the U.S. Department of Education, is a nationwide system of information centers, each responsible for a given educational level or field of study. ERIC's basic objective is to make developments in educational research, instruction, and teacher training readily accessible to educators and members of related professions.

The **ERIC Clearinghouse on Languages and Linguistics (ERIC/CLL)**, one of the specialized information centers in the ERIC system, is operated by the Center for Applied Linguistics (CAL) and is specifically responsible for the collection and dissemination of information on research in languages and linguistics and on the application of research to language teaching and learning.

In 1989, CAL was awarded a contract to expand the activities of ERIC/CLL through the establishment of an adjunct ERIC clearinghouse, the **National Clearinghouse for ESL Literacy Education (NCLE)**. NCLE's specific focus is literacy education for language minority adults and out-of-school youth.

ERIC/CLL and NCLE commission recognized authorities in languages, linguistics, adult literacy education, and English as a second language (ESL) to write about current issues in these fields. Monographs, intended for educators, researchers, and others interested in language education, are published under the series title, Language in Education: Theory and Practice (LIE). The *LIE* series includes practical guides for teachers, state-of-the-art papers, research reviews, and collected reports.

For further information on the ERIC system, ERIC/CLL, or NCLE, contact either clearinghouse at the Center for Applied Linguistics, 1118 22nd Street, NW, Washington, DC 20037. Internet e-mail: ncle@cal.org. You may also wish to visit CAL's Website at http://www.cal.org.

Joy Kreeft Peyton, Fran Keenan, Series Editors
Vickie Lewelling, ERIC/CLL Publications Coordinator
Miriam J. Burt, NCLE Publications Coordinator

Other LIE Titles Available from Delta Systems

The following are other titles in the *Language in Education* series published by the Center for Applied Linguistics and Delta Systems Co., Inc.:

Adult Biliteracy in the United States (ISBN 0-937354-83-X)
edited by David Spener

Assessing Success in Family Literacy Projects: Alternative Approaches to Assessment and Evaluation (ISBN 0-937354-85-6)
edited by Daniel D. Holt

Immigrant Learners and Their Families: Literacy to Connect the Generations (ISBN 0-937354-84-8)
edited by Gail Weinstein-Shr and Elizabeth Quintero

Literacy and Language Diversity in the United States (ISBN 0-937354-86-4)
by Terrence G. Wiley

Making Meaning, Making Change: Participatory Curriculum Development for Adult ESL Literacy (ISBN 0-937354-79-1)
by Elsa Roberts Auerbach

Talking Shop: A Curriculum Sourcebook for Participatory Adult ESL (ISBN 0-937354-78-3)
by Andrea Nash, Ann Cason, Madeline Rhum, Loren McGrail, and Rosario Gomez-Sanford

Writing Our Lives: Reflections on Dialogue Journal Writing with Adults Learning English (ISBN 0-937354-71-6)
edited by Joy Kreeft Peyton and Jana Staton

To order any of these titles, call Delta Systems, Co., Inc. at (800) 323-8270 or (815) 363-3582 (9-5 EST) or write to them at 1400 Miller Pkwy., McHenry, Illinois 60050 (USA). Visit Delta Systems on the World Wide Web at http://www.delta-systems.com.